You Can't Be Serious

You Can't Be Serious

James Martin

The Pentland Press Limited
Edinburgh • Cambridge • Durham • USA

© James Martin 1995

First published in 1995 by
The Pentland Press Ltd.
1 Hutton Close
South Church
Bishop Auckland
Durham

British Library Cataloguing in Publication Data.
A catalogue record for this book is available
from the British Library.

ISBN 1 85821 288 X

Typeset by CBS, Felixstowe, Suffolk
Printed and bound by Antony Rowe Ltd., Chippenham

Introduction:

Resurrection – Fact or Fiction

My own journey into personal Christian faith was eventually by way of agonizing wrestling with the question of whether or not it was possible to believe in the Resurrection of Jesus as a historical event. I was sixteen years old and had been feeling with increasing force that God was calling me to serve Him in the Christian ministry.

At the same time I was being assailed with serious doubts about the historical credentials of the Christian faith itself, particularly with regard to its centrepiece, the claim that Jesus had been raised from the dead. Could such an extraordinary thing possibly be true? Was not the whole idea absurd and impossible? If so, was not the very structure of Christian belief destroyed?

For me at that point, this was the most crucial question that had ever confronted me. Was the Resurrection of Jesus fact or fiction? For many months this question was my constant and decidedly uncomfortable companion.

In the end I emerged from my period of very painful mental conflict with a firm conviction that the Resurrection must be fact not fiction. I could find no other explanation that would fit the evidence with any real measure of satisfaction.

The following pages attempt to reflect something of the battle that was waged within my mind as it strove, determinedly but unsuccessfully, to discover a satisfactory alternative explanation for the Resurrection belief. I have endeavoured to put my questionings of that time into the form of letters I might have written to my minister about my problem

1

if only I had not been too diffident to do other than have the battle fought out in the secret places of my own mind. I accompany them with the kind of letters of reply I might write now to someone making similar enquiries of me.

Dear Minister

I must confess that, a bit to my surprise, I quite enjoyed attending your church service when I was back home for a spell last month, although – to be honest – there were parts of the service that bored me to tears. Some of the hymns, for instance, are a bit of a turn-off so far as I am concerned. Your sermons, however, are pretty interesting most of the time, perhaps because you do not make them too long.

I found it rather much on my last Sunday, however, when you were preaching about Easter. Since I will not be back home again for some months, this is what has prompted me to write.

You gave the impression that you really believed the story that Jesus was raised to life again after being crucified to death. Surely you can not be serious. After all, that story is so ridiculous by modern standards. No one should be expected to believe it nowadays. It might have been all right in Palestine in the first century but it will not do for our scientific modern age. Dead people simply do not come back to life again and I must say that I do not think you do the Christian cause much good by claiming that Jesus did. To make such an obviously absurd claim will just turn people away from the church. There are a lot of good things in Christianity. I would suggest, with respect, that you should concentrate on them in your preaching and leave out any reference to Jesus' Resurrection.

Yours,

John

Dear John

I am glad that you are enjoying some parts of our church service. Perhaps if you keep coming you will begin to enjoy it even more and may even encounter some hymns that turn you on.

But, of course, what you were primarily writing about was your inability to accept the story of Jesus' Resurrection as historical truth. Let me tell you that I understand how you feel and have some sympathy with you. But as for giving up referring to the Resurrection or ceasing to preach about it, that is just not possible. The belief that Jesus was raised from the dead at the first Easter is at the very heart of the Christian message.

What is more, surprising as it may appear to you, I do really believe in its truth myself. My conviction is not just a matter of blind, unreasoning faith. The reason I so well understand your reaction about what seems an absurdity to you is that in my youth I used for a time to feel exactly the same about the Easter story, regarding it as a stupid fairy tale which no sensible person could possibly believe. But I came to see that there were a whole lot of things in favour of belief in the Resurrection, things which could not easily be dismissed and which, in the end, convinced me.

Like you, at one time I found it well-nigh impossible to entertain the truth of the Resurrection as a serious possibility because it seemed so blatantly obvious that such an event simply could not have taken place. As you put it, dead people do not come back to life again. I came, however, to recognize that it is less than scientific to proceed on the bland assumption that this is not only normally the case but must always be the case regardless of any evidence to the contrary. I came to recognize further that there is a mighty lot of evidence to support the claim that Jesus was raised from the dead. There are many strands of evidence and clearly any attempt to dismiss the Resurrection as mere myth requires to offer alternative (and satisfactory) explanations of these. I was forced to the conclusion that the only truly satisfactory explanation of the various strands was that the Resurrection was a historically true event.

You say that no one should be expected to believe the Resurrection story *nowadays*; but I say that nowadays it is not permissible to rule anything out of court without reference to whatever evidence may be available. I ask you, therefore, not to reject completely the possibility of the Resurrection being true until you have given the relevant evidence a real chance; and there is a lot of it, I assure you. We believers have a strong case.

Yours sincerely

Dear Minister

I do not need any more convincing that you are serious in your Resurrection belief; but I will need a great deal more convincing that the belief is founded on truth. I am certainly not going to accept without demur all your glib talk about there being a lot of evidence for it. Generalities of that nature do not cut any ice with me. You will need to be much more specific. How about citing just one item of your 'strong' case for a start?

Dear John

I take your point. I am afraid it is a temptation that most ministers fall prey to at some time or another, to talk in generalities when their people want and need – and deserve – something more specific.

Well, then, here is something to start with. Have a think, if you will, about the evidence provided by the New Testament. Here are various first-century writers, of different backgrounds and different temperaments, writing at different times and from different standpoints, and all agreeing in their testimony that Jesus of Nazareth, who was crucified to death under Pontius Pilate, was raised to life again three days later. Is that not evidence of considerable significance? Would it not form pretty formidable evidence even by modern standards? Would the concerted testimony of so many independent witnesses not be likely to prove conclusive in any present-day court of law?

Have a think, particularly, about the testimony provided by the writers of the four gospels and Paul and Peter, for these six write more explicitly about the Resurrection event. Here are six men who were entitled to speak with authority about that event because each of them in their various ways had intimate knowledge of the first Easter either because he had been there in person or because he had derived his information from those who were. They were, therefore, in a position to be sure that what they had to say was in accord with the facts.

None of them, I admit, had actually seen the Resurrection taking place – no one had – but I suggest to you that it is nevertheless compelling evidence that all of them are in agreement that Jesus came back to life at the first Easter after being well and truly dead on the first Good Friday, and that quite clearly the claim they made was in harmony with what the whole Christian church believed and had believed from the beginning.

Perhaps that is enough to begin with. I will leave you to reflect on it. Here are six men whom there is no reason to regard as other than honest and reliable. What is more, they were in a position to speak with authority on the subject. They assert in their independent fashion that Jesus was raised from the dead. That is not something that can be lightly set aside, is it?

Dear Minister

I was inclined at first to be considerably impressed by the way you cited the united testimony of the New Testament writers to the Resurrection of Jesus. I was almost tempted to raise my hands in surrender and say, 'All right. You win. It must be true.' But that was only for a moment. I realized the very next instant that there were flaws in your argument.

For a start, is it not the case that the New Testament books were written a long time after the alleged events of the first Easter? You can't seriously expect me to allow to such testimony the same weight as you are claiming for it. There must have been so much likelihood during the gap of time of inaccuracies creeping in, as to render the testimony more or less worthless.

Dear John

I could not disagree with you more when you suggest that the time lapse between the Easter events and the writing of the New Testament books must seriously impair the value of their testimony to the Resurrection. There is a whole lot I would like to say in an effort to help you understand better the position in regard to these books. I hope you will bear with me.

To begin with, let me say a word or two about Paul's letters, which speak so emphatically about Jesus being raised from the dead. In the course of his missionary travels and as a result of his intimate personal relationship with many of the young Christian churches, Paul must have written a great many letters dealing with matters of faith and conduct and of church order and discipline. Some of these letters have survived and are now part of our New Testament. These letters were written within the four decades following the death and Resurrection of Jesus and at times incorporated material that was much earlier.

They indicate very plainly that Christians had believed from the beginning of the church that Jesus was risen, and Paul himself subscribes wholeheartedly to that belief.

I would like to draw your attention to one particularly interesting section in Paul's First Letter to the Corinthians. I will quote it to save you having to look it up: 'I passed on to you what I received, which is of the greatest importance; that Christ died for our sins, as written in the Scriptures; that he was buried and that he was raised to life three days later, as written in the Scriptures; that he appeared to Peter and then to all twelve apostles. Then he appeared to more than five hundred of his followers at once, most of whom are still alive, although some have died. Then he appeared to James and afterwards to all the apostles. Last of all he appeared also to me.' This passage is to be found in chapter fifteen, verses three to eight.

Now, this letter was written around AD 55 which was only some 25 years after the Resurrection took place or, as you might prefer to say, was supposed to have taken place. Paul says that he 'passed on' what he had received. In other words, his preaching to the Corinthians in regard to the Resurrection was in the first instance the relaying of a message which was neither his invention nor his theorizing but which had been given to him by the Christian church through some of its members and given, it seems safe to presume, at the time of his conversion. This we know to have occurred no later than AD 35. That is to say, Paul's message of the Resurrection of Jesus which he received with the authority of the church and which he later passed on to the people of Corinth and of which he now gives them reminder, goes back to a mere handful of years after the first Easter.

Not only that. It was not even a case of this message of Jesus' Resurrection having been *discovered* by Paul in AD 35. That was when he came to believe in it but the message itself and the belief in it had been on the go long before that, ever since the first Easter in fact. This means that there simply were not the time nor the opportunity that you assumed there were for a false message of Resurrection to arise or for the truth of a permanently dead Jesus to be distorted into the lie of a risen Christ. Because, you see, the story that Jesus had been raised from the dead was what brought the Christian church into being and it was continuously being told and retold in that church from the outset of its history.

What Paul was testifying to in his letters, what the rest of the New Testament testifies to as well and the story of Jesus that Matthew, Mark, Luke and John put into their gospels, was something that was so integral to the life of the Christian church and so much a part of it from the beginning onwards as to leave without any foundation your suspicions of possible inaccuracies developing.

Dear Minister

I must say that I am quite unconvinced. The fact remains that the gospels which are the main sources for the Easter story and claim were written a considerable time after the Easter events they purport to describe. The Gospel of Mark, the scholars inform me, was the earliest to be written and even it was not penned until at least AD 60. Surely that represents a gap of time long enough for memories to become dulled, for errors to intrude and for legends to develop.

There is this, also, to be remembered: all the New Testament writers, including the four evangelists, were committed to the Christian faith. They can scarcely, therefore, be regarded as unbiased witnesses. I cannot agree that the New Testament provides such strong evidence for the Resurrection as you maintain.

Dear John

Let me take your last point first.

The fact that the authors of the New Testament books, and of the gospels in particular, were Christians does not alter the undoubted circumstance that they were men in a position to know the truth about it and who affirmed that the Resurrection was true.

It is the case that all the earliest written evidence for the Resurrection is supplied by people who believed in it; but it would have been a very remarkable circumstance if it had been otherwise. In these early years only those who believed in it would have found any occasion to write about the Resurrection or to refer to the still very small and, to outsiders, apparently very insignificant body of Christian believers.

Your main point, however, is that the time lapse between the first Easter and the gospel narratives must render the credibility of the narratives suspect. I could reply, and I do reply for starters, that anyone with a personal involvement in a dramatic and important event may well be hazy about the details if writing down the story 20, 30, 40 or even 60 years afterwards but is not likely to be in doubt as to its main outline.

I need not rest my case there, however, for the manner in which the gospels came to be written was itself a safeguard of their essential accuracy. In the main the story of Jesus, including that of his Resurrection, was transmitted by word of mouth down the years that intervened between his life on earth and the compilation of the four canonical gospels. There was some writing down of the story much earlier, perhaps even in the form of some diary notes while Jesus was still alive, but nothing of a very systematic nature was produced prior to the gospels. The reminiscences of Jesus which eventually were in them were mainly preserved and perpetuated by oral transmission.

That statement, John, may appear to concede your point that the accuracy and credibility of the gospels' account must, therefore, be suspect. Quite the reverse. Let me attempt briefly to explain just why I should say that.

We of the Western world are so accustomed to the printed word that we intend to regard as markedly inferior anything that depends entirely or even largely on oral tradition. It was far from being like that in the world of Jesus' day and of the emergence of the gospels. The Jewish people of that time prized oral tradition above the written word, especially when it was known to have been passed on by the mouths of those who were in a position to do so with authority and trustworthiness. That, as a matter of fact, is why the four gospels did not arrive on the scene until the eyewitnesses of the Jesus' events were becoming thin on the ground. It was then that the Christian church felt it would be wise and good to have some record of the more important of these Jesus' events committed to the more permanent vehicle of writing while there were still surviving those who had been eyewitnesses and who could, therefore, ensure that what was written down was in full accord with the facts as they knew them to be.

Not only so. The power of memory and, consequently, the accuracy of verbal transmission among the Jews were of a phenomenal nature by our Western standards although commonplace in the East. The Jews mostly learned and taught by word of mouth. Their very word for instruction, 'mishnah' is literally translated, 'repetition', which suggests the learning by heart that was the regular custom. From the beginning they showed great aptitude for this and, allied to long practice, it produced memories of remarkable accuracy. Exactly the same is true of other Eastern countries like India where the training of verbal memory has long been regarded as of great importance.

In addition to this phenomenal power of memory that the Jewish people possessed and exercised there were other factors safeguarding the accuracy of the transmission of the Jesus' story during the 'oral years', things like the unbroken continuity of the tradition and its public nature. As a result, I am personally totally convinced that when the time came for Mark, Matthew, Luke and John to write their gospels, the mass of oral reminiscence from which they selected the bulk of their material was substantially as it had first been recounted at the outset. Here were four men who, if not themselves eyewitnesses, had personal access to those who were. After carefully sifting the material, both oral and written, which the Christian church possessed concerning Jesus, and whose substantial accuracy cannot reasonably be doubted, they wrote the four little books that we know as the gospels. In these gospels all four devote a prominent place to the claim that Jesus was risen from the dead. Would you not agree that this comprises evidence that is difficult to set aside?

Dear Minister

It is not good enough just to say 'other factors like the unbroken continuity of the transmission and its public nature'. You will have to explain what you mean.

Dear John

Point taken. Here goes.

When I speak of the unbroken continuity of the oral transmission, I mean that the story of the Resurrection, in common with the other reminiscences of Jesus which eventually found their way into the gospel records, was handed down continuously during the mainly word-of-mouth period between Easter and the emergence of these records.

It is quite at variance with the facts of the case to imagine, as some critics seem to do, that immediately after Easter the Resurrection story was placed in some kind of cold storage and only thawed out for general consumption when the gospels came to be written, forty or more years later. The actuality was quite different. The stories of Jesus' life and teaching and especially of his death and resurrection, were constantly being told and retold during the years that elapsed between the (supposed) events of Easter and the appearance of the gospels.

Not only so. That constant telling and retelling was not merely the concern of a limited number but the concern and activity of the whole church. This is what I mean by its public nature. These stories of Jesus were the basis both of worship and of evangelism. They were repeated over and over again as Christians met together for worship and as they went seeking to persuade others to join them in following Jesus.

This constant reiteration in a public fashion of the historical truths that were the foundation of the Christian faith ensured that they were preserved accurately. Any attempted deviation, whether deliberate or accidental, from the universally known and accepted version of these facts would have been met with an immediate outcry of protest that would have been sufficient to secure speedy correction.

That is what I meant when I claimed that factors like the unbroken continuity and public nature of the oral transmission of the Jesus story were safeguards of its accuracy.

Dear Minister

There is a further point about the forty-year gap between the life of Jesus and the first written gospel. I have a decided feeling of unease about the length of that gap. If they were so convinced of the importance of Jesus and of his Resurrection, why did they take so long to put it down in writing? I would have expected that if Jesus had really risen from the dead and they knew about it, they would have been rushing to put something about it down on paper (well, parchment, wasn't it?) as quickly as possible. Isn't the delay itself cause for suspicion? After all, if something even half as startling as a resurrection occurred today, there would be a book out about it tomorrow or the day after, would there not?

Dear John

Your last sentence pinpoints where you are going wrong, as many do, I may say, in your estimate of the significance of the gap of time between the life of Jesus and the compiling of the gospel records. It all hinges upon the vast difference in regard to books that exists between our modern times and first-century times in Palestine.

The invention of printing was then, of course, many centuries in the future and every book had to be written out by hand, as had every copy of it. This was not only a laborious and time-consuming process, it was also very expensive. Difficult as it may be to appreciate, accustomed as we are to printing presses churning out masses of books every day, in the first century books were a rare commodity.

What is more, in the Palestine of Jesus' day, books ranked inferior in status to the spoken word, especially if that word was spoken by someone of known authority.

In the early years of the Christian church, therefore, there was neither need nor desire for written records like the gospels. There were plenty of people around who had the authority to tell the story of Jesus, including a number who had even been his companions and eyewitnesses of the events involving him. That is not to say that there was not some writing down of the things Jesus had said and the things he had done. It was, however, spasmodic and fragmentary. The spoken testimony was what mattered most.

It was then, as I have indicated already, only with the passage of time and the thinning of the ranks of those who had actually known Jesus in the flesh that the need was felt to produce some kind of systematic written record while there were still eyewitnesses on hand to give their approval to the finished work. So it was that there came into being the four little books that stand now at the beginning of the New Testament. In the writing of them the authors, since time and expense limited the size of their books, made very careful selection of the material available to them, so that what resulted were in a way official and officially vouched-for testimonies. The delay in time between the close of Jesus' earthly life and the writing of the gospels, far from being surprisingly long, was in the circumstances of the time just what was to be expected.

Dear Minister

I am prepared to admit that you are fighting a good corner on behalf of the accuracy of the oral transmission of the Resurrection story but I am certainly not yet ready to admit that you have won the contest. What about the contradictions to be found in the gospels? For instance, when I read them, I find that they do not always agree with one another and sometimes they seem to contradict each other quite startlingly. How can that possibly be squared with your claim that they are to be taken as trustworthy records?

Dear John

You are putting up a pretty good fight yourself; and you are perfectly correct when you say that there are differences and even contradictions between the various gospel accounts of Jesus' Resurrection. Unlike you, however, I see these features as confirming the honesty and reliability of the writers rather than casting doubts upon their testimony.

Supposing they had all tallied exactly in every detail, would you have found them more convincing if they had? I rather think not. For my part, if the four gospel accounts of the Resurrection story had been identical, I would have been forced to suspect collusion and even a doctoring of the narrative in order to eliminate possible difficulties. As things are, the presence of differences seems to me to give a clear indication that each of the four writers dealt with his sources with scrupulous honesty, recording the story as he knew or believed it to be without any attempt to remove any inconvenient items.

If there had been any tampering with the Jesus' reminiscences as handed down in the church, whether deliberately or inadvertently, nothing seems surer than that the difficult and apparently contradictory elements would have been modified or omitted. The existence of such elements in the narratives speaks volumes for the faithfulness and respect with which the evangelists treated the materials of Jesus – reminiscences that came to them.

What we have in the four gospel records of the Resurrection is just the kind of thing I for one would expect to be provided by four honest men giving an honest report concerning a very exciting and very important event. Supposing you were to ask four spectators of a very exciting football match each to write his or her version of the event, you would be likely to find their accounts show a number of differences, sometimes quite astonishing differences, of detail. But if the reporters were honest and reliable, you would also find them agreeing on the essential features, including the final score. That is the kind of situation we find reflected in the gospel narratives of Jesus' Resurrection –

differences of detail, even contradictions, but a united testimony to the fact that the Resurrection actually happened.

We have to bear in mind, you see, that if the Resurrection really took place then the disciples must have been in a state of extreme excitement. We could hardly expect them in such circumstances to keep careful diary notes of every detail or even to retain an explicitly clear mental picture of everything that occurred. Remembering that and remembering, too, that each of the writers gives his testimony from his own point of view and that none of them professes to give an exhaustive account, we ought not to be surprised that differences occur, sometimes quite marked differences, in the detail of the narrative.

Here is an illustration that may help to make my point clearer. A history class was studying the French Revolution and was asked to do some research on the vote by which Louis XV was condemned to death. When the class handed in their reports, it was discovered that nearly half the class said the vote was unanimous, a fair number said there had been a majority of one and a few said that the majority was 145 out of a vote of 721. At first sight, these reports might appear so contradictory as to cast doubt on the whole affair, even though all were agreed that Louis was condemned. But in fact all were true. The full story was that three votes were taken at his trial. The first was on the question of Louis's guilt and the vote was unanimous. The second vote was to determine the penalty and a majority of 145 voted for death. The third vote which had a majority of one decided that the sentence should be carried out at once.

Your own experience is likely to furnish you with illustrations of a similar nature. Mine does at any rate. When, for instance, I find my diary recording for a certain morning, 'worked at sermon from 9 to 12.30', but making no mention of the telephone call received at ten o'clock nor of the cup of tea I drank at 10.30, does that make it an unreliable record?

No, John, the variations we meet in the gospel records of the Resurrection seem to me not to detract from but rather to add to the unmistakable ring of authenticity sounding through them and serve to confirm my belief that they reflect originally eyewitness accounts which have been handed down in largely uncorrupted form through the years of oral transmission.

Of course, as I have tried to argue earlier, it should come as no surprise that this should be so when we take into account the various factors at work to safeguard that accuracy. Remember, for instance, that the tradition was not simply the prerogative of a few individuals but the property of the whole church which regarded it not as a museum piece but as a living entity, using it regularly in its worship and in its missionary activity. Remember, too, that right up to and including the time of writing the gospels, there were people around who had actually been with Jesus.

I would like to add this comment. Even if you regard the gospel narratives with the deepest suspicion, it still remains absolutely certain that from the outset of the Christian church the whole body of Christians believed that Jesus had been raised from the dead. Nobody would or could dispute that. May I ask you how you would propose to account for the origin of that belief if Jesus had not been raised?

Dear Minister

You ask how I might account for the Resurrection belief if, in fact, it never took place. Frankly, I do not think you have set me a very difficult exercise, never mind an impossible one, as you seem to think. Sorry to disappoint you but several possible answers to your question come to my mind.

One very real possibility, it seems to me, is that the whole thing was a gigantic fraud. The disciples of Jesus were so disappointed that what had seemed so glorious an enterprise should have come to such an inglorious finish that they decided to manipulate history in order to keep it going. They determined that the crusade of love and righteousness which Jesus had begun should not after all come to an end on a Roman gallows; and so they agreed to put about the story that he had been raised from the dead.

Don't you think it could all have started like that? I certainly think it could.

Dear John

Sorry to disappoint *you* – well, not sorry really – but there are a number of very serious objections to be brought against your theory that the Resurrection belief might be no more than the result of a fraud perpetrated by the disciples of Jesus. It sounds all very well at first – the most gigantic hoax in history, etc. – but it does not stand up under serious examination, as I hope to show you.

In the first place, the character of Jesus and the high moral standards that he taught his followers are surely enough in themselves to exclude any possibility that they could have founded a church in his name on the basis of a deliberate fraud. In view of the incontrovertible fact that Jesus expected his followers to be thoroughly honest and truthful, is it even remotely credible that they could have started the whole thing off with a fabrication and gone on to build up the church on a known lie?

Even if somehow they had been so minded, is it any more credible that a sheer invention on their part could have produced the results that ensued in them? If they had made up the story, do you think it at all conceivable that they could have shown such enthusiasm for it as they did, even to the point of being willing to suffer and to die for it, as many of them did. And how could a known lie of their own invention have made them into the changed men they undoubtedly became?

In any event, it is highly unlikely that the disciples could have got away with such a fraud to the astonishing extent that they did. Apart from anything else, it must have involved a lot more than agreeing among themselves to tell a story of Resurrection. It required a high degree of skilful planning. Were that company of apparently average intellects capable of the feat of meticulous organization that must have been involved?

Another thing, they needed to tell their story so persuasively that it convinced a whole lot of other people, many of whom were sceptical or even hostile. Is it, I ask you, credible that they could have managed to do this, especially in Jerusalem so soon after the alleged events where it would have been so easy to pick holes in any made-up story since the supposed facts of their claim were capable of such ready scrutiny and investigation, the empty tomb for example?

And this is to say nothing of the difficulty of understanding how not one of those in the know spilled any of the beans later on despite the opposition, the interrogations and the persecution they had to endure because of it.

Dear Minister

I agree that in the light of the ethic that Jesus taught, it is not a reasonable possibility that his followers could have initiated a Jesus cult on the basis of a deliberate fraud perpetrated by themselves.

Nevertheless, accepting their sincerity, might they not have been deluded? Granted that it was not a trick, could the Resurrection claim not have been a genuine mistake on their part? Loving Jesus so much as they did, so disappointed as they were to see him killed, could they not somehow have managed to persuade themselves that he had come back to life again?

You see, a dead man coming back to life again is so extraordinary an event that I am very loath to believe that it ever happened. I am sure there must be some other explanation of the belief and I wonder if self-delusion could be the answer. In their emotional distress after the crucifixion, I imagine it might not have been all that difficult for them to fancy that Jesus had come back to life again.

Dear John

I well understand your feeling when you say that the Resurrection is so extraordinary a happening that you feel compelled to search for an alternative explanation. I must, however, say that your suggestion of a self-induced delusion on the part of the disciples will not do either. It runs counter to the facts of the case at several points.

Without going into these at the moment, let me ask you if it is all likely that so many people as were involved at the beginning could have been individually deluded? Even if we were to allow that possibility, that would be far from ending your problems so far as this particular theory is concerned. You would now have to account for the failure of the many, and able, opponents of the new faith and its Resurrection belief to expose it for the glaring error it was. As I said in my last letter, this would have been the easiest of tasks in that place and at that time if the Easter story was some kind of mistake. What could have been simpler, for instance, than to point out where the dead body of Jesus lay in its grave? That would have burst the Christian bubble right away.

Dear Minister

I find it difficult to resist the arguments you have put forward against my suggested theories of fraud or delusion to explain the rise of the Resurrection belief. At the same time I am reluctant to abandon the idea of it somehow or other having originated through error. Could it be, perhaps, that it is to be explained by reference to the legends of dying and rising gods that were, I understand, not unknown in the Eastern world of that time?

What I am getting at is this: since such legends were current at the time, would it not have been quite natural for the followers of Jesus to evolve a similar legend of their own concerning the founder of their faith? That is to say, is it not at least a possibility that – not right away but after a while – there crept into the story of Jesus the belief that after he was crucified God raised him to life again?

Dear John

I have to say that your latest suggestion that the Resurrection belief may have been a legendary growth fails to impress me.

To begin with, and this in itself deals your theory a knock-out blow, there was neither time nor opportunity for the kind of legendary development you suggest. You say 'not right away' but unfortunately for your theory, the Resurrection belief did arise right away. Every legend requires time, usually considerable time, for its growth. They do not, and they cannot, spring up overnight like mushrooms do. The belief that Jesus was raised from the dead came into being only three days after his death.

Now, if events had taken a different course, if, say, following the crucifixion no word of resurrection was heard for a period of some years and then the story began to circulate that Jesus was risen, in such circumstances we might very well have suspected a legend born out of little or no historical foundation. Since, however, this Resurrection belief was formed immediately after the crucifixion and public proclamation of it was being made in the streets of Jerusalem no more than seven weeks later, there simply was no time for the intrusion of legend.

I think I ought to point out also, contrary to what you have been informed, that there is no evidence whatsoever for thinking that the first Christians moved in an environment where legends of dying and rising gods were current. There is no doubt that there were such legends in the Greek and Mediterranean world; but Christianity emerged from a Jewish background. By far the majority of the early Christians were Jews and the influences to which their thinking was exposed were those of orthodox Judaism and the Old Testament in particular. Such influences would not incline them in favour of any legend of resurrection, rather the reverse.

In any case, no known example of a dying and rising god legend offers anything like a close parallel to the Resurrection of Jesus. It is true that the Hellenistic world contained numerous legends of gods who were supposed to have died and risen again. But without exception these were recognized as belonging to the realm of mythology and were never in any danger of being taken as historical fact. There is no known example of belief in the resurrection of a historical person such as Jesus was.

Dear Minister

I have not changed my view that there simply must be some reasonable alternative to accepting the Resurrection story. Anything seems preferable to believing that this extraordinary event – one without any parallel in all history – actually took place. You said earlier on that you yourself had been very sceptical about it at one time but that you had been overpowered by the weight of evidence in its favour. Frankly, I do not think any amount of evidence could convince *me*. I feel that there is simply no place in the scheme of the universe for such an unnatural event to be possible. It seems to me that no matter how much evidence you might marshal in its favour, any explanation other than the Resurrection of Jesus is to be preferred.

All the same, I am still perfectly willing to give careful consideration to whatever else you have to say on the subject.

Dear John

I appreciate your willingness to consider what I have to put forward in favour of the truth of the Resurrection. I fully realize that no one can be entirely free from bias or prejudice and we are all in danger of locking our mind into set and immovable positions. It is far from easy to succeed in being open-minded about matters on which we have already formed strong opinions.

That being so, I appreciate all the more your readiness to be as fair as possible in your assessment of the case I am trying to promote; and I would encourage you in that readiness by reaffirming that in this modern age we are not properly entitled to rule out any alleged historical fact on a priori grounds. The only legitimate question concerning any such allegation – and this applies as much to the Resurrection claim as to anything else – is whether or not the evidence justifies us in accepting it as true.

On that basis I submit for your consideration, as a beginning, the fact of the empty tomb. The grave in which the dead body of Jesus was laid to rest on the evening of the first Good Friday was discovered to be empty on the following Sunday morning (Easter Day). The fact of the grave's emptiness is generally accepted and I suggest to you that the reason this has never been seriously disputed is that it would simply not be reasonable to do so. After all, those on the spot who were hostile to the emergence of the new Christian faith, and there were many such, could find nothing better to say regarding the report of the empty tomb than that the disciples had stolen the body. Such a claim, plaintive though it is, is a clear admission of the emptiness of the grave.

That being so, dear friend, my position is that there is no satisfactory explanation of the tomb being vacant other than that Jesus had been raised to life again as his disciples said.

Dear Minister

With respect, it seems to me that there are several quite feasible explanations of the empty tomb other than accepting that Jesus was raised from the dead. I content myself with mentioning only one to begin with.

How about that explanation quoted in the New Testament itself and to which you have yourself referred, namely that the disciples stole away Jesus' body under cover of darkness and then spread abroad the story that he was risen from the dead? Don't you agree that might be what really happened? After all, this was what those opposed to the Christian claim asserted right at the outset. May this not be the real truth of the matter? Desperate to keep their leader's work going, his followers removed his body secretly, left the grave empty and then proceeded to build up the church.

Dear John

You are a bit like a terrier with a bone but it won't do. If you have not already thrown it out, I would like you to refer to a previous letter in which I attempted to demonstrate the untenable nature of any theory involving deliberate fraud on the part of the disciples. For them to steal the body and then make out that Jesus was risen from the dead would require them to act in direct contradiction to the kind of moral behaviour Jesus had constantly advocated. To suggest that their devotion to Jesus might persuade them to further his cause by becoming tricksters is to forget that that very devotion would ensure that they remained obedient to his high ethical standards and render this kind of deception unthinkable.

That apart, it is rather naïve to imagine that they could have got away with stealing the body. It would have involved a brave and extremely well-organized operation to open up the grave and make off with Jesus' corpse without anyone apparently either seeing or hearing them, and all this despite the presence of a guard at the tomb. A remarkable enterprise of this nature does not seem likely to have been within the compass of the group of men who comprised the band of disciples. Furthermore, it involved not only succeeding in accomplishing this without being detected but also succeeding in keeping the real truth of the matter a complete secret so far as anyone outside their immediate small circle was concerned. All of these requirements seem beyond the bounds of reasonable expectation. Equally so, if this were the way of it, is the astonishing fact that not one of them was ever constrained to divulge the true story despite all the hardships and persecutions they had to endure in later years.

In the light of these considerations, I put it to you that no theory of removal of his body by the friends of Jesus can reasonably be entertained.

Dear Minister

In view of your comments I must admit that I now find it no longer an attractive theory that the friends of Jesus removed his body secretly from the tomb and so started the Resurrection story. But I am not finished. There were other human hands that might have been responsible for the removal of the body. What about Jesus' enemies? He had, as you yourself pointed out, plenty of them in Jerusalem at that time and they were exceedingly anxious to suppress any interest in him. Isn't it possible that they could have been responsible for the grave being found empty on the first Easter morning? They could well have decided to remove the body, for example, in order to prevent possible veneration of the tomb and the remains it contained.

They had been anxious to have Jesus put to death. That accomplished, they were no doubt more than a little annoyed that he had been given an honourable burial, instead of what was usually an executed felon's lot, and may well have been afraid that his tomb would become an object of pilgrimage. In order to avoid this possibility, it seems to me not at all unlikely that they should have decided to remove the body from its grave.

Your perfectly valid arguments against removal by the disciples – the improbability of deliberate dishonesty on their part and the practical difficulties confronting them – do not apply in the least where Jesus' enemies were concerned. So how about this?

Dear John

You sound so enthusiastic about your latest attempt to account for the empty tomb in a less than supernatural way that I am almost sorry to have to tell you that it will not stand up to close scrutiny any more successfully than your previous one.

It is indeed true that those hostile to Jesus would not be faced, as the disciples would be, with moral scruples in connection with the abstracting of the body from the tomb. Nor would they face the same practical problems in the removal. But reflect on this, John. If they had removed the body, it must have been for the purpose, as you suggest, of preventing possible veneration of the grave and consequent perpetuation of the name of Jesus. Well, then, don't you think that as soon as Jesus' followers began to noise abroad their message that Jesus was risen, the first thing the removers of his body would do would be to shout out loud and clear, 'Hold on. Jesus' grave is empty because we moved his body. He is still very dead and we can show you his corpse to prove it.' If they had done that, it would have halted the Resurrection preaching in its tracks.

But they signally failed to do any such thing. I can think of nothing to explain their failure except total inability to take that course of action. It is perfectly obvious that they could have had no part in the removal of Jesus' body from the tomb and no idea where the body had gone, otherwise the whole of Jerusalem would have been informed without delay.

Dear Minister

I think I may have got it this time.

I have come across a book which contains the suggestion that Jesus was not really dead but only comatose when laid in his tomb. There, in the coolness, he recovered consciousness, made his escape and rejoined the disciples to inspire them with a belief that he had been raised back to life. I find this theory very attractive and it would solve a lot of problems for me. Not only does it do away with the supernatural element which, as you know, is what I find most difficult to stomach but it strikes me as being very plausible. It is an explanation which seems to me to fit the facts of the case very well.

Would you not agree that it is at least possible that it was in this way that the tomb was left empty and the story of Jesus' Resurrection given its origin?

Dear John

The theory you have come across of Jesus being not dead but only in a fainting condition when placed in the tomb so that he was able to revive and escape and give the disciples the impression that he had come back to life is interesting but by no means new. It was put forward first as long ago as the beginning of the nineteenth century. It was speedily discredited then but it keeps reappearing every now and again in some book or article written by someone who thinks he has unearthed a startling new alternative to the Christian believer's understanding of the meaning of the empty tomb.

But it will not do. Let me try to explain why.

To begin with, the first requirement of this theory – usually referred to as The Swoon Theory, by the way – that Jesus was not really dead when laid in the tomb is one of the utmost improbability. Having previously been scourged, an ordeal of such severe lashing as was enough to cause the deaths of many who were subjected to it, Jesus was then impaled on the cross for some six hours, after which he was taken down and pronounced dead. It was part of the task of the execution squad to make sure that the condemned person had truly expired. In view of the well-known ruthless efficiency of the Romans, the fact that those responsible for the execution of Jesus were satisfied that he was dead would seem to leave no room whatsoever for the possibility that, despite all he had undergone, there was still life left in him.

However, let us suppose for the sake of argument, you and I, that Jesus was not dead but merely in some kind of swoon condition when taken down from the cross and laid in Joseph of Arimathea's tomb. What the Swoon Theory now asks us to believe is quite extraordinary. Try to imagine what had to be involved.

Arrested the previous evening, Jesus had been up all night and during that time had been subjected to severe verbal attacks involving severe mental and nervous strain. After this had come an interrogation by the Roman Governor culminating in the dreadful blood-letting and strength-sapping punishment of the flagellum, (a many-thonged whip whose thongs were studded with sharp pieces of metal and bone that were calculated to tear the flesh from the victim's body) prior to being led out to the place of crucifixion. Already so weakened that he was unable, as was customary, to carry his own cross to the execution site, Jesus was then nailed to that cross and left stretched out on that horrific instrument of death to endure six hours there in the mounting heat of the day.

To verify his death a spear was run through his body before Joseph and Nicodemus were given permission to see to his burial. Before they laid him in the new, rock-hewn tomb of the rolling stone type belonging to Joseph, they observed the normal pre-burial custom of wrapping the body round and round with many yards of linen inlaid with a hundred-pound weight of spices. This done, the body was placed on a ledge inside the tomb and a massive circular stone was propelled along the groove fashioned in the rock outside the tomb so that it lay across the entrance sealing if off completely from the outside world.

What The Swoon Theory asks us to believe is that this Jesus, who had approached so near to death without actually dying and who must at the very least have been in a seriously weakened condition as a result of his sufferings and his loss of blood, somehow regained consciousness and somehow, despite his weakness, struggled free from the mass of linen enswathing him and after that, although having to work from the inside of the tomb where it would be extremely difficult to obtain any kind of purchase on the heavy stone, somehow managed to roll back the stone and make his escape.

This proposition does not seem credible to me. How about you?

Let us carry our consideration of this theory a step further. Let us, for the sake of argument, suppose that all this highly improbable scenario was in fact played out and that the once comatose Jesus, now revived, made his escape from the tomb. Think for a moment, John, what The Swoon Theory now demands of our capacity to believe.

It asks us to believe that such a returned Jesus – naked, weak and practically helpless – inspired his followers with a conviction that he had conquered death. Not, mark you, that he had survived death but that he had *conquered* it. There is not a shadow of doubt that the belief that Jesus had conquered death was at the very heart of the disciples' future ministry. Is it possible to imagine that such a refugee from the grave, as The Swoon Theory represents Jesus to be, could have persuaded his disciples that he had overcome death not merely escaped it?

After all, if Jesus had somehow recovered in the tomb and escaped to rejoin his disciples, he must have needed medical treatment and nursing care. Moreover, he must eventually have died for real. Could such a person instil in the disciples the certainty that undoubtedly possessed them that Jesus had triumphed over death?

Perhaps you will allow me, John, to try to summarize the position regarding the empty tomb. As I – and many others – see it, it is a major piece of evidence for the truth of the Resurrection. It is a stubborn piece of history on the rock of which many sceptical assaults have been broken; for the empty tomb can find no satisfactory explanation for itself except that Jesus was raised from the dead.

Please forgive me for going on so long about The Swoon Theory but I find it a fascinating study and I hope I have said enough to show you that it has nothing to commend it.

I will give you time to digest this rather long letter before I ask you to consider the appearances of the risen Jesus which is the next factor in the evidence that I intend to cite.

Dear John

Here, as promised, is what I want to say to you about the appearances of the risen Jesus.

The discovery of the empty tomb would not of itself have produced a belief that Jesus had been raised from the dead. By itself that discovery would have produced only bewilderment and confusion, which are the very reactions it did produce in the beginning, as the gospel narratives reveal. But something else occurred in the experience of the disciples which supplied them with the key to the true significance of the empty tomb. That something was that they saw the risen Jesus.

Bear in mind that in the first century books had to be produced individually by hand and were, therefore, very expensive to make. One consequence of this was that the four gospels were of necessity small books, able to contain only a small selection of the material available. No doubt there were more appearances of the risen Jesus than are recorded but Christians should be grateful that the New Testament nevertheless mentions no fewer than ten.

You might find it of some interest if I tell you where they are to be found.

> John 20: 1-18 (paralleled in Mark 16:9) tells of the risen Jesus appearing to Mary Magdalene beside the tomb in the garden.
> Matthew 28:1-10 tells of an appearance to a group of women in the garden.
> Luke 24:34 and 1 Cor. 15:5 tell of an appearance to Peter.
> Luke 24:13-31 (with a parallel reference in Mark 16:12-13) tells of Jesus appearing to two people on the road to Emmaus.
> John 21:1-14 describes how the risen Jesus appeared to seven of his disciples on the shore of Lake Galilee.

1 Cor. 15:7 mentions an appearance to James.

There are four other appearances recorded, in each case to the eleven apostles and other followers. The Bible references are:

i) Luke 24:34-79, John 20:19-23, 1 Cor. 15:5, Mark 16:14-18
ii) John 20:24-29
iii) Matthew 28:16-20, 1 Cor. 15:16
iv) Luke 24;50-53. Acts 1:3-9, Mark 16:19-20

On these recorded occasions and almost certainly on a goodly number of others Jesus appeared alive after his crucifixion. First of all, on the very same day as his tomb was found empty, he was seen and spoken with by a number of his friends and thereafter over the next six weeks this happened again and again, sometimes involving one individual, sometimes a group and on one occasion five hundred all at once. I submit to you, John, that this is testimony to the reality of the Resurrection that must be taken seriously, so seriously indeed that there is no way it can be accounted for unless Jesus was raised from the dead.

Dear Minister

I will not attempt to contest the incontestable, namely that the disciples genuinely believed that they had seen Jesus alive after his Resurrection. At the same time, while the reality of their belief may be in no doubt, the reality of the appearances themselves may well be a totally different matter. It seems to me that they might perfectly reasonably be explained otherwise.

Far from seeing Jesus risen from the dead, it strikes me as being much more likely that the disciples and their associates were suffering from hallucinations; and that the so-called 'appearances' were no more than figments of their imaginations. They were so convinced that their leader could not be defeated that they confidently expected him to come back from the grave. This expectation took such hold of them that they came to imagine that they had actually seen him. It probably started with Mary Magdalene. Going to the burial garden at dawn on Easter morning, she met someone there and imagined it was Jesus. That experience was enough to spark off a whole series of hallucinations. After she had rushed to tell the disciples that she had seen Jesus risen, he was soon being 'seen' here, there and almost everywhere.

I am afraid your case for the truth of the Resurrection rests on a pretty flimsy foundation so far as this piece of alleged evidence is concerned. What are claimed to have been appearances of the risen Jesus may be easily accounted for in the way I have described, nothing more than the product of overheated imaginations.

Dear John

Your argument for regarding the appearances of the risen Jesus as figments of excited and expectant imaginations is well put and carries a measure of superficial attraction. I must insist, though, that its attraction is no more than superficial. Once it is examined closely, it is seen to have fatal flaws.

For one thing, the disciples did not possess the expectation of Jesus' Resurrection that this theory demands. It is the primary prerequisite of any experience of hallucination that the recipient should be expecting to see what he comes to fancy he sees. In the case of the supposed appearances of Jesus this essential condition was not fulfilled. The disciples were *not* expecting the Resurrection, far from it. The indisputable fact is that the crucifixion took them by surprise and left them crushed and broken, in despair and entirely without hope. The leader round whom they had woven such dreams and of whom they had expected such great things in the future had been put to death in ignominious fashion. They were utterly shattered. Jesus had failed and failed miserably. All they were concerned about now was to save their own skins. Their mood was quite the reverse of that needed to produce visions of a Jesus raised from the dead. They were only too brokenheartedly sure that they would never see him again.

As a matter of fact, far from being in a state of mind that would make them ready subjects of such a hallucination, they were decidedly reluctant to accept the fact of Jesus' Resurrection even after he had appeared to them in risen form. Here was no group of men only too ready to snatch at straws and quick to embrace any suggestion that Jesus was alive again. On the contrary, when the women came to the disciples with their news of his Resurrection, they were met with disbelief and scorn, as we read in St Luke's Gospel, 'the apostles thought that what the women said was nonsense, and they did not believe them' (chapter 24, verse 11).

One of them at least continued to be sceptical even after the risen Jesus had shown himself to the rest. John's Gospel's narrative of the first Easter night has this to say, 'One of the twelve disciples, Thomas (called the twin), was not with them when Jesus came. So the other disciples told him, "We have seen the Lord." Thomas said to them, "Unless I see the scars of the nails in his hands and put my finger on those scars and my hand in his side, I will not believe."' (chapter 20 verses 24 and 25). And in Matthew's Gospel (chapter 28 verse 17) there is recorded, 'When they saw him, they worshipped him, *even though some of them doubted.*'

By the time the gospels came to be written the disciples were held in such high regard throughout the Christian church that such uncomplimentary references to them could never have found their way into what were almost official records unless they had been absolutely true to the facts of the case. And they make it as plain as can be that far from being anticipated, the Resurrection of their Leader took the disciples so much by surprise that their first reaction was one of incredulity.

You might want to come back at me here, since I know you have been spending a lot of time reading the Gospels, so let me anticipate your rejoinder. I fancy that you are at this point wanting to jump in and say, 'Hold on, old man. Didn't Jesus prophecy that he would rise from the dead? Surely that would be enough to create in his disciples' minds an expectation of his Resurrection? How do you square that with your declaration that they were not expecting it?'

Clearly Jesus did try at times to foretell his Resurrection to his disciples. Just as clearly they persistently failed to understand him on this point. Even in the gospels, written as they were with the full light of Easter illuminating the events and sayings of Jesus, even there what he had to say about his forthcoming Resurrection is neither very explicit nor very prominent. This surely indicates how little his utterances about the Resurrection were grasped at the times they were spoken. Whether the explanation is that Jesus refrained deliberately from making his language too definite at this juncture or that it was a case of the idea being too strange and too difficult for them, the fact remains they do not seem to have cottoned on to what he was telling them.

The second of these explanations seems to me to be the more probable. The disciples refused to take Jesus seriously when he attempted to warn them of his impending death and to prepare them for it. Since they were slow and reluctant to understand that part of his teaching, how could they possibly grasp his teaching concerning the resurrection that was to follow? Certainly Jesus' endeavours to acquaint them with what lay ahead for him proved largely unavailing so that when the blow fell and the crucifixion came, it took them unawares and left them desolate.

At the very real risk of making this letter into a long essay, or even a lecture, I would like to go on to point out some aspects of the appearances of the risen Jesus that are extremely difficult to square with any suggestion that these appearances were no more than hallucinations.

Hallucinations are invariably the product of nervous minds and communicated by suggestion to other nervous minds. The disciples do not in the least fill this particular bill. They do not emerge from the gospels as people who are in any danger of falling prey to hallucination, rather the reverse. I suppose it could fairly be argued without smacking too much of male chauvinism that it might be possible to draft the women in Jesus' party into the role of hallucination victims; but the men whom the hallucination theory requires also to play their part can not be so coerced. In the main a stolidly practical and unimaginative lot, they are far from being likely subjects of hysteria and fanciful flights of imagination.

That is one aspect I would like you to consider. Here is another. The circumstances of the post-Easter appearances of Jesus do not conform with what a hallucination explanation would lead us to expect. There is no hint of mass suggestion, with the fantasy of one highly strung mind being multiplied in others. Instead we have a number of appearances that occur independently, to different individuals or groups, at different times and in different places.

There is this point, also. Hallucinations usually are momentary phenomena; but the appearances of Jesus are not mere fleeting glimpses. Quite often he stays with his friends for a considerable period of time.

Moreover, John, the normal pattern of hallucination experiences is that they become increasingly extravagant and increasingly numerous. So far as the appearances of Jesus are concerned, the picture is much different. These are, all along, remarkably restrained in character and they quite fail to follow the usual pattern of a feverishly mounting frequency over a considerable period. On the contrary they cease altogether after about six weeks. Not only that, they come to an abrupt cessation, whereas hallucinations usually run a fever-like course, rising to a peak and then tailing gradually away.

There is this further feature of the appearances which merits consideration. The effect they had on the minds and on the behaviour of the disciples is the opposite of that which hallucinations would be expected to produce. Hallucinations tend to leave their subjects enervated, exhausted and apathetic. The disciples, on the other hand, were left clear-headed in their belief about Jesus, purposeful in obeying his commands and enthusiastic in telling others about him.

Once again I must apologise for writing such a long letter; but once again my defence must be that this is not only a fascinating subject but an important one.

Dear Minister

I am prepared to admit the validity of the points you make against the likelihood of the appearances of Jesus after his Resurrection being understood in terms of hallucination.

I am wondering, all the same, if there may be some kind of halfway house. I have come across a theory propounded by a theologian called Theodor Keim a century ago which refers to the appearances as 'telegrams from heaven'. Keim accepts that the appearances can not legitimately be explained as merely subjective experiences like hallucinations but wants to stop short of allowing them the fully objective character assigned to them by orthodox Christian belief.

Keim, therefore, proposes a middle course. His suggested explanation of the appearances is that, although the body of Jesus slept on in its grave, his spirit survived and imparted to the disciples mental images of him risen which assured them that he had conquered death –

objective visions that were 'telegrams from heaven'. When the disciples 'saw' the risen Jesus, they were not simply imagining fantasies bred in their own minds but were seeing something that although immaterial had a reality outside of themselves.

Dear John

Keim's theory was, and is, a rather curious one. It avoids the impossible situation of trying to maintain that the appearances were no more than subjective images but in its attempt to remove the supernatural from the narrative, it succeeds only in replacing it with one that is equally supernormal. I find it difficult to understand how Keim and his friends should regard his 'telegrams from heaven' as easier of belief than the orthodox understanding of the appearances.

In any event, the postulating of God-given visions rather than hallucinations is a theory that founders no less completely than the other on the nature of the facts it is required to explain. The character of the appearances and the witness of the New Testament concerning them refuse to be tailored to a shape that will fit Keim's specifications; and, of course, there is still the basic fact of the empty tomb which can not be accommodated to any theory of hallucinations or mere visions, whether subjective or objective.

Dear Minister

My reading of the gospel narratives and our discussions about the appearances of the risen Jesus prompt me to raise with you the question of the nature of the risen body of Jesus. This seems to me a substantial obstacle in the way of believing in the Resurrection. You see, I find it extremely difficult to understand what that risen body is supposed to consist of. The narratives do not furnish anything like a coherent picture and that is enough to make me sceptical of their trustworthiness. In one instance, the risen Jesus seems to be tangible and in another he suddenly appears in the presence of the disciples despite their being behind locked doors.

How can you possibly make sense of that sort of thing? And if you can not – and I certainly can't – does not that throw the whole concept of Jesus' Resurrection back into the realm of severe doubt?

Dear John

You raise a very interesting subject when you express your puzzlement about the exact nature of Jesus' resurrection body. I have to confess that it puzzles me, too. I hope I have been able to answer with some degree of satisfaction at least some of the questions you have brought up in the course of our discussion by letter but I have to admit that I will not be able to offer you anything like a complete answer to this one. I do not know what the risen body of Jesus consisted of and I can not begin to explain it.

There are some comments I would like to make, nevertheless, comments which I believe are to the point. The first is that the truth or otherwise of the Resurrection of Jesus is really independent of our ability to understand or explain the nature of his risen body. This may strike you as all too obvious but I felt it was a point worth making. If Jesus did rise from the dead, then whether or not I comprehend what his risen body was like does not alter the truth of that event any more than my inability to understand exactly how the sun exerts attraction on the earth alters the fact that it does.

Here is another point worth keeping in mind. There is no good reason for thinking that our limited human understanding ought to be able to comprehend the nature of that risen body. Even before his Resurrection, Jesus, although subject to what may be referred to as the laws of nature, was able to use these laws in ways that even now we can not repeat and often can not understand. There is no good reason for us to think of him as being more limited afterwards.

Despite what I have just been saying, I am willing – for what little it may be worth to you – to share with you my own rather unsuccessful wrestlings with this problem. I started from the premise that I should seek a theory to fit the facts and not be misled into trying to fit the facts in a preconceived theory. Otherwise I might well have concluded at the outset that the risen body of Jesus must have been either physical or phantasmal, that is, either flesh or spirit. To choose either of these categories, I came to see, would be to force myself into doing violence to the known facts.

The true explanation would seem to lie somewhere between these two clearly defined and intelligible categories, for it has to take account of these three major facts: i. the tomb was left empty; ii. the risen Jesus displayed physical attributes, viz. he was visible, audible and tangible; iii. the risen Jesus displayed non-physical attributes, viz. he was able to appear and disappear at will.

Personally, I am able to go no further in attempting any definition of the composition of Jesus' resurrection body. I content myself with borrowing from St Paul and describing it as a 'spiritual' body without being very clear in my own mind as to what exactly I mean by that, except that I certainly do not mean something that was pure spirit as opposed to pure matter. I think I mean that somehow in the Resurrection the physical body of Jesus became the perfect unhindered vehicle of his spirit and no longer subject to the limitations which were necessarily there in his pre-Resurrection life on earth.

What I am attempting to say, in what I am aware is very stumbling fashion, may well offer you no help at all; but this way of looking at the matter has been of some help to me. It does not explain how Jesus' body during the post-Resurrection period displayed both material and non-material characteristics but it does make it easier for me to accept the apparent contradictions. The important thing, as I see it, is that what appeared to the disciples was really Jesus and not a disembodied spirit; and yet what they saw was different from his body of flesh and superior to its laws.

Another way to speak of Jesus' Resurrection body might be to describe it as 'glorified' and this may, indeed, enshrine even more effectively the double idea of continuity and transformation which seems to me inherent in the whole story of the post-Resurrection appearances. In other words, it was still Jesus but it was neither merely a resuscitated corpse nor a mere ghost. The body that had been laid in the tomb was gathered up into the risen Jesus but in a wonderfully changed condition.

Dear Minister

I will need to read your last letter more than once, I think, in order to get hold of it properly and so I will not comment upon it at the moment. Perhaps I'll come back to it later. Meantime, just to let you see how open-minded I am, let me mention a feature of the Resurrection story which strikes me as a point in favour of its truth. I have been much impressed in my reading of the narratives by the quite astonishing change that took place in the disciples over the first Easter weekend. Between the Friday and the Sunday they became totally different persons and the transformation would appear to be very, very difficult to explain apart from a belief in the Resurrection of their Leader. What do you feel about this?

Dear John

I was so delighted to receive your last letter; and particularly to learn of your reaction to the transformation effected in the disciples over the first Easter weekend. I could not agree more when you remark that this would seem to be very difficult to explain apart from a belief in the Resurrection of Jesus. I would even go so far as to say that this transformation can not reasonably be accounted for except on the basis of that Resurrection belief being founded on fact. It seems to me to be a psychological miracle which demands the miracle of the Resurrection to explain it.

The change that occurred in Jesus' disciples that Easter weekend was one of the most dramatic and most spectacular that has ever occurred in any individual or any group. The Friday of the crucifixion left them utterly crushed and broken. They had centred such high hopes round Jesus and had come to expect so much of him; and now he was dead. Even worse than that, he had been put to death by crucifixion. Anyone who knew his Bible was well aware that this was conclusive evidence that Jesus could not have been the Messiah they had latterly come to think he was.

The Bible stated quite uncompromisingly that anyone who suffered death by crucifixion was under God's curse. St Paul says in Galatians 3:13, 'Anyone who is hanged on a tree is under God's curse', referring back to the statement in Deuteronomy 21:23 to that effect. No thought of Jesus being Messiah could survive in any Jewish mind once he had been crucified. Consequently, the disciples were not only dismally aware that they had lost for ever one who had been a wonderful friend and leader but in addition they were left in no doubt that they had been sadly misguided in thinking that he was the promised Messiah. Clearly if he had been the Messiah, God would never have permitted him to end up as he did on a Roman cross.

This realization compounded their distress so much that it would be hard to imagine a more sorry bunch than they presented after Jesus had been executed. Sad of heart, desolate and disillusioned, they were floundering that Good Friday evening amongst the shattered remains of their hopes and dreams. The fine, brave enterprise on which they had been engaged with Jesus had come to a shocking end. All that was left for them now was to try and save their own skins. As a result, they spent the weekend skulking behind locked doors, fearful that the next approaching footfall might herald the approach of the high priest's gestapo come to hale them off to share their leader's fate. They were longing for the Sabbath (Saturday) to be over, with its travelling restrictions, so that they might get out of Jerusalem and return to their old haunts and their former occupations, there to lick their wounds.

That was how they were on the Friday night and through the Saturday. But by the close of the weekend they were scarcely recognizable as the same people. Their brokenheartedness had been transformed to joy; their despair had been transformed to confident hope; and their craven fear had been transformed to lion-hearted courage. The transformation was so remarkable that only their discovery that Jesus was alive again can account for it with any degree of satisfaction.

You have put your finger upon one of the strong strands of evidence for the historical truth of the Resurrection. The disciples were so astonishingly changed from what they had been on Good Friday night that some extraordinary experience must have befallen them to cause the change. They said it was because Jesus had been raised from the dead and they had become aware of it. What else could it have been?

I put it to you, John, that nothing else offers a satisfactory explanation of their transformation. I put it to you, also, that nothing else offers a satisfactory explanation of the existence of the Christian church. Easter Day was the birthday of the church and without the Resurrection the church would have been stillborn.

Dear Minister

I see now how foolish I was to give you the advantage of admitting how profoundly impressed I was by the change that took place in the disciples over Easter weekend. Not content with elaborating on that, you go and throw in the existence of the church as another major piece of evidence for the truth of the Resurrection. But I am not going to take that lying down.

As I see it, it is perfectly possible that the church could have been founded by the followers of Jesus for no other reason than that they loved him and wanted to perpetuate his name and his teaching. I am not in the slightest prepared to concede that it needed the miracle of Jesus' Resurrection to bring his church into being. Admitting that it is difficult to account for the transformation of the disciples apart from Jesus' Resurrection is one thing; agreeing that the existence of the church demands that Resurrection is quite another.

You will need to explain yourself a bit more fully here.

Dear John

I am only too willing to take you up and try to indicate why the very existence of the Christian church speaks strongly in favour of the truth of the Resurrection.

If there had been no Resurrection, if the dead, crucified body of Jesus had been the last his followers saw of him, there is no doubt at all that at the first opportunity they would have made their way back to their own homes and their old way of life. They would, no doubt, carry with them some nostalgic memories of the stirring, thrilling, inspiring times they had shared with the young preacher from Nazareth and, perhaps, also some sorrowful yearnings for the days that were irretrievably gone.

But any such thoughts would be of things that were past and done.

Heavily overlaying them would be their recollection, their all too vivid recollection, of the terrible finish to the story and of seeing Jesus spreadeagled on the cross before being laid lifeless in his tomb. At times, perhaps, when in one another's company, they might hark back to the years they had spent with Jesus but they would take very good care not to speak of Jesus or of their association with him to anyone who had not been his follower. For this would be to invite scorn or anger and might even lead to retribution of one kind or another.

As for preaching about Jesus and attempting to promote some kind of Jesus cult, even if they had felt any desire to do such things, they would not have dared embark on such a harebrained scheme. That could have been to put themselves in serious jeopardy. In any case, what did they have to preach? The only story they had to tell was one of stark tragedy and unmitigated defeat. And as for suggesting to others that they should align themselves with Jesus and seek to follow his teaching, that would have been quite absurd. The man turned out a failure in the end, didn't he, and he was now dead and gone. Who would want to be interested in him?

Had there been no Resurrection, there seems little doubt that events would have run a course like that. Little mention would ever again have been made of Jesus of Nazareth once his crucifixion was past. There would have been, could have been, no preaching of the Gospel because there would have been no Gospel to preach. 'Gospel' means literally 'Good News' and their only news was bad, news of abject disappointment, awful failure and irretrievable defeat.

Everyone knows that the actual course of history was much different from the scenario just outlined. Shortly after the sorrow and the heartbreak of Jesus' crucifixion, his followers blazed into a very fire of fearless action. Instead of being returned to the anonymity of their old haunts and their old jobs, history finds them banded together in an evangelical crusade with its starting off point in the very city where Jesus had been put to death, taking every opportunity to persuade others to follow Jesus, not as a dead hero but as a living Friend and

Saviour.

On the one hand we have the picture of what seems bound to have happened if Calvary had been the end of Jesus; on the other hand we have the story of what actually did happen. It is my belief that only the Resurrection can adequately explain the turn of events.

Dear Minister

I am still not altogether persuaded that it was impossible for the disciples to have started up the Christian church even without Jesus having been raised from the dead. It is amazing what people can do sometimes if they are determined enough and this, I think, may have been a matter of his friends being determined enough that Jesus and his teaching should not be forgotten.

Dear John

I can't help feeling that you are beginning to whistle in the dark.

I've already tried to point out how extremely improbable it is that Jesus' disciples could have sought to perpetuate his memory and found his church unless they had been totally convinced that he was risen from the dead; and very few people will have any doubt concerning the sincerity of their belief in that Resurrection. Setting aside that point for a moment, it is absolutely certain that the proclamation of the Resurrection was at the very centre of the first Christian preaching. I would like you to ask yourself how that preaching could have made any impact whatsoever, especially in Jerusalem at that time of all times, if it had not been based on incontrovertible historical fact.

Unless it was so based, is it even remotely possible that it could even have got off the ground so soon after the alleged event in the very place where it was supposed to have happened? Not at all, I would say.

If the Resurrection had not taken place and if, for instance, the body of Jesus lay rotting in its grave, it would have been the easiest thing in the world surely for those hostile to Jesus – and there were plenty of them around – to expose the falseness of the claim and so to prick the bubble of the Resurrection claim right at the outset. Jerusalem was a small city and all that was needed was for someone to say, 'This claim is arrant nonsense. I can show you where the body of Jesus lies', and that would decidedly have been that.

I suggest to you, John, that the fact that this was not done can be accounted for only on the assumption that it *could* not. Look at it this way. If the Resurrection was not true, then Jerusalem was the worst place in the whole world that could have been chosen as the location for the starting up of the Resurrection preaching, the place where it would have been most easily exposed for the lie it was.

You could say that when the preaching of the Resurrection began, Jerusalem was like an arena in which were two contending sets of gladiators, one trying its best to promote belief in the Resurrection, the other trying its best to demolish it. On the one side were the priestly authorities and their henchmen, who had been implacably opposed to Jesus and his teaching and were now just as implacably opposed to the claim that he was risen from the dead. They numbered in their ranks some of the country's keenest intellects and finest debaters. The Resurrection story was sure to be investigated from every angle and in an ultra-critical spirit. Any weakness was sure to be exploited to the full. If not true, what chance of survival did the Resurrection claim have in Jerusalem at that point in history where evidence of its falseness must be lying to hand and where it was confronted by opposition of such a deadly nature? Against the priestly side, with its lawyers well versed in the use of argument and the science of debate, stood only a small group of rather ordinary people, a few with some education but most with little. On the face of it, the odds were all in favour of the priestly faction and yet they lost the contest. How could they possibly have lost unless the cause they were opposing was founded on truth?

The situation in Jerusalem in those early post-Easter times presents an even more remarkable and even more significant picture than I have so far outlined. For the newborn Christian church did not merely survive, it grew and prospered. In other words, it was not merely a matter of the case for the truth of the Resurrection being too strong for its enemies to disprove, it was strong enough to convince many who started out by being either sceptical or indifferent. The church in fact gained ground at a quite astonishing pace. In little more than a generation it had spread far beyond the country of its origin and had reached out to Asia Minor, Greece and even Rome, the then mistress of the world, counting its adherents no longer in scores but in scores of thousands.

It is inconceivable that the Christian cause and case could have achieved such phenomenal growth if its central message of the Resurrection of Jesus had been false. And, remember, those who were won to the new faith in those early days were not naturally conditioned to lap up a story of Resurrection like this. Their prejudices were such, whether they were Jew or Gentile, as would markedly predispose them against believing the claim being made by the Christian preachers. These preachers must have been constantly subjected to intensive interrogation and searching cross-examination regarding their startling message and the evidence they could adduce to support it. Given the circumstances that obtained, the astounding number of converts they made speaks for itself.

Particularly this is so with regard to the progress of the infant Christian church in *Jerusalem*. The public proclamation of the Resurrection in that city began only a few short weeks after the career of Jesus had come to an end on a gallows in that very place. Many of the people in Jerusalem to whom the first missionary preaching was addressed would actually have seen Jesus in his death-throes and all of them would be well acquainted with his story. The crucifixion must have seemed to every Jew – as it seemed to the disciples in the beginning – to be indisputable proof that Jesus had been a fraud, certainly so far as any thought of his being Messiah was concerned. These Jerusalemites were very close to the events both in time and in place so that for them much of the Resurrection story was open to direct personal investigation. Moreover, the Jewish authorities, who exerted considerable influence upon the mass of the people, absolutely denied the Resurrection and obviously would employ every means to attack the disciples' claim and expose any apparent point of weakness in it.

In view of all this, it seems to me – and I hope it may be as clear to you – that the story which persuaded anyone in Jerusalem that Jesus had been raised from the dead had to be one that could stand up to the most thorough investigation. That thousands of converts were made there in the first few weeks of the church is, I think, impossible to explain unless the story of Jesus' Resurrection was founded on solid historical fact.

Dear Minister

I am compelled to admit that the origin and survival of the Resurrection-based Christian church in Jerusalem where it all had taken place, and then its rapid expansion there, is very impressive and hard to account for unless the Resurrection was true. I wonder at the same time, however, if there has not been a bit of lily-gilding in the New Testament accounts of the upbuilding of the church. I read in Acts (chapter 6, verse 7), that 'a great number of priests accepted the faith'. That surely can not be taken as accurate reporting. The priests were so diametrically opposed to the faith that it is highly unlikely that any of them, never mind 'a great number' of them, could be persuaded by any means to accept it.

Wouldn't you agree that overstating the case like this merely weakens it?

Dear John

No, I do not agree, for the simple reason that I do not regard Acts as having overstated the case as you assert. I am firmly of the opinion that Acts could not have included such a statement unless it had been true to the facts.

Quite apart from the fact that Luke (author of Acts as well as of the Gospel that bears his name) is generally held in high regard as a reliable historian – and he tells us himself in the opening verses of his Gospel that he took considerable pains to assess all the available testimony before committing that Gospel to paper – it is difficult to see how such an extraordinary statement could have been made unless it had the backing of known truth.

I fully agree with you on this point, that the conversion of a number of priests is not at all what one would have been expecting. The unexpectedness of it, however, seems to me to be an indication of the probable accuracy of the report rather than the reverse. Had it been fiction, it would never have been countenanced as deserving a mention.

Its unexpectedness not only is a confirmation, to me at least, of its being a piece of accurate reporting but also furnishes a further piece of evidence for the truth of the Resurrection. Deeply impressive as it is that the Resurrection belief found acceptance – against the odds – in the minds of many 'ordinary' inhabitants of Jerusalem in the early days, it is even more impressive that it should capture the allegiance of some priests. They were, of course, bitterly hostile to the new sect; and they were 'in the know'. That is to say, they possessed all the information available to the anti-Christian side and were acquainted with all the anti-Resurrection arguments and counter-explanations.

Predisposed in so many ways to reject the Christian claim, these priests were perhaps the least likely people in all history to be persuaded that the Resurrection story was true. Yet many of them were. Can this be explained except on the basis of the case for the Resurrection being so convincing that only obstinate refusal to face the facts could resist it?

Dear Minister

So far as the conversion of the priests is concerned, I take the points you make in your last letter. I must ask, nevertheless, if you would not feel compelled to agree that the reference to 'a great number of priests' being converted may be too vague to have as much impact as evidence as you would like. What I am getting at is that we do not know anything about these priests as individuals. It could be that there were personal reasons for making them more open to persuasion than their colleagues. Perhaps they were of an inferior mental calibre, for example, or for some reason not so well versed in the opposing view. If we knew some personal details about even one of them, that might make this particular piece of testimony all the more effective. It is a pity from your point of view that you are unable to supply any, is it not?

Dear John

I am not sure whether or not you had your tongue in your cheek when you wrote your last letter but there is one person moved to belief in the Resurrection of Jesus from an originally hostile position about whom quite a lot is known. I refer to Saul of Tarsus who became St Paul, the great missionary apostle of the early church. His conversion to faith in the Resurrection and the risen Jesus is more than just a minor factor in assessing the weight of evidence in favour of the Resurrection.

Saul of Tarsus, a staunch upholder of all things Jewish and extremely learned about his Jewish religion, a 'Pharisee of the Pharisees' to use his own phrase, was bitterly hostile to the new Christian faith. He hated it with every fibre of his being and his hatred was fuelled by his horror at what he considered to be an awful blasphemy, the claim of the Christians that Jesus, a crucified felon, had been raised from the dead. A man of unusual intellectual gifts, for a lengthy period of time he devoted his many talents to the attempted extermination of the Christian faith. By his own desire he became the official persecutor-in-chief of the Christians and spared no effort to harry and destroy them. He was without doubt the very last person anyone could have expected to become a Christian, but he did, making a turnabout that astonished everyone. If you care to look up Acts chapter 9, especially verse 21, you will be able to grasp something of the extent of the astonishment his volte-face caused. It must have taken a very convincing case for the Resurrection to prevail on such a one as Saul of Tarsus to come to believe in it.

His eventual acceptance of the Resurrection belief assumes even greater significance when we take into account the circumstance that his intense hatred and untiring persecution of the Christian sect were allied to his having access to all the information and all the counter-explanations available to the high-priest and his colleagues. A Pharisee himself and occupying the major role he did in the campaign against the adherents of the Easter faith, Saul would inevitably be fully acquainted with all the facts of the case as known to the priestly headquarters and be well briefed in all the means employed to refute the absurd allegation that Jesus had been raised from the dead. Intellectually as well as emotionally, he was strongly predisposed against the Christian claim. Then, suddenly and sensationally, he turned completely round. He set out from Jerusalem to go to Damascus and root out and eliminate the Christian colony which was known to be there; but by the time he arrived in Damascus he was thoroughly convinced that he had been wrong and the Christians had been right all along. So convinced was he now of the truth of the Resurrection faith that soon he was to be found launching himself upon one missionary crusade after another in the promotion of the very Christian faith he had once so violently persecuted.

What actually happened on the road to Damascus, apart from the cardinal fact that Saul had a vision of the Risen Christ, is a matter of some difference of opinion. This 'appearance' of Jesus to Saul, if we give it that name, was clearly different in some respects from the earlier post-Easter appearances. Saul, however, was in no doubt that what he had seen possessed independent reality. He firmly believed that the risen Jesus had actually made himself visible to him; and also, despite the obvious differences, he had no hesitation in adding this event to the list of Resurrection appearances that he listed in 1. Corinthians, chapter 15. On Paul's own understanding of his Damascus Road experience, its significance as evidence for the Resurrection is on a par with that of the appearances to the disciples earlier on.

If, on the other hand, the vision was a purely subjective experience, as some scholars interpret it, having reality only in Saul's mind, its significance as evidence is scarcely less. The crucial point is that, if it were a subjective vision, it could not have come about unless Saul had been forced to the conclusion that the story of Jesus being raised from the dead must be true. It had to be very persuasive evidence that produced such a change in Saul of Tarsus. It had to be so overwhelming that even this Pharisee of the Pharisees with all his predisposition to unbelief could no longer hold out against it.

The conversion of Saul, the resolute and militant unbeliever, to Paul, the committed believer, is such a remarkable phenomenon that I am going to crave your indulgence as I attempt to emphasize its significance by underlining four features of the case.

For one thing, keep in mind that Saul of Tarsus was a man of outstanding intellectual stature, by general consent one of history's intellectual giants. He was also a man of considerable learning. His was no unthinking, uncritical, credulous mind that could be easily captured. Here was one who was able to sift evidence, to assess experiences and to subject alleged facts to searching scrutiny. Such a man as Saul was not likely to be ensnared by a faith that rested upon deception or mistake.

Secondly, exceptionally ardent Pharisee that he was, Saul's whole training and background were such as to set him in opposition to the very idea of the Christians being right. The mere suggestion that a crucified man could be Messiah was outrageous blasphemy to him. That is part of the reason for his venting such violent hatred on the Christians. He regarded them as blasphemers and deceivers. Such a man would accept the Resurrection belief only if he were left with no alternative.

Thirdly, it is worth noting that Saul's conversion was no half-hearted thing. It was not merely a case of him beginning to think that there was a possibility that he was wrong; he became utterly convinced that *they* were right. He did not simply cease to criticize and persecute; he began to commend and evangelize. Just as thoroughly as he had been against Christianity, so now he was for it. His conversion was the thorough-going affair of a man who was sure beyond all shadow of doubt.

Fourthly, Saul's conversion was not only complete, it was enduring. When Saul changed his ground on the Damascus Road, he changed it for ever. The new course he charted then was one that he followed all the rest of his life, even though it was to cost him dear in terms of hardship and suffering. It led him into much pain and trouble – into ridicule, hatred, persecution, stoning, flogging, shipwreck, imprisonment, martyrdom. The man who was prepared to endure all this for the sake of a faith he had once despised must have been very, very sure that it was based on a firm foundation.

Dear Minister

I am still some way off being totally convinced about the Resurrection but thanks to you I can see there is indeed a strong case for it. I have at the same time found it very interesting to read the New Testament again in the light of our discussions. One or two particularly interesting points have emerged from my reading on which I would like to have your opinion.

Here is one. Although Christianity had its roots in the Jewish religion where the holy day, the Sabbath, was and is Saturday, the Christian holy day is Sunday. That seems strange. How did it come about?

Dear John

The point you raise about Sunday becoming the holy day for Christians is interesting in itself. It also, in a minor way, may offer additional confirmation of the truth of the Resurrection.

You are perfectly correct, of course, in stating that Christianity emerged from Judaism. Jesus, its Founder, was himself a Jew and most of his early followers were Jews. It would seem natural, almost inevitable, that the Christian church would continue to observe the Sabbath as the holy day of the week, the day nearly all of them had been accustomed to treating as their special day for rest and worship. That it settled on Sunday instead of Saturday was for the reason that Sunday was the day of its Lord's Resurrection.

The first Christians, coming as they did from the ranks of Jewry, did, to begin with, continue to observe the Sabbath worship they were used to; but very soon they began to meet together on Sundays as well for their own distinctive worship. In Acts, chapter 20 verse 7, for instance, we read, 'On the first day of the week, when we were gathered together to break bread.' The Jewish day was then, as still, reckoned from sunset to sunset and this gathering together of the Christians would take place after sunset had ended the Sabbath and brought in the first day of the week (Saturday evening to us but Sunday by their reckoning). At first this would be their only free time on a Sunday which was a normal working day. Gradually, however, worship on the first day of the week completely took over from Sabbath worship, so far as the Christians were concerned.

Why did this happen? Why did they change from the familiarity of the Sabbath as the day of worship? This was a very remarkable thing to happen in view of the fact that the earliest Christians were nearly all Jews and converted Jews continued to form a large proportion of the Christian church all through the first century. Only some very outstanding consideration could have induced them to inaugurate such a change. Could it have been anything other than their conviction that it was on the first day of the week that their Leader, Jesus, had been raised from the dead? That was what made Sunday such a special day for them.

Additional significance may be found in the fact that it is the Book of Revelation which designates the first day of the week, the Sunday set apart for Christian worship, as 'The Lord's Day' (chapter 1, verse 10). This book was written in Asia Minor where Emperor-worship was prevalent and strong, including a monthly festival in his honour that was called 'Emperor's Day'. This festival seems to have been a monthly commemoration of the day when the Emperor acceded to the throne. The irresistible conclusion would seem to be that the application of the title, 'the Lord's Day', to Sunday – by this time, late in the first century, universally recognized by the Christians as their day of worship – was a very pointed reminder that this was the day of their Lord's accession, the day that he had been raised from the dead.

Let me quote you a couple of sentences from a great Scottish divine of the past. James Denney was his name and he was a Professor in Trinity College, Glasgow, a long time ago. In one of his books he says 'Every Sunday as it comes round is a new argument for the Resurrection. The decisive event in the inauguration of the new religion took place on that day – an event so decisive and sure that it displaced even the Sabbath' (*Jesus and the Gospel*, p 113).

While I am at it, I may as well say something about this title 'Lord' that the early Christians assigned to Jesus. That, too, I think, is not without significance in relation to the Resurrection belief. From the very beginning of the Church, the followers of the new religion not only called Jesus 'Saviour', they also called him 'Lord'. This was to accord him equal status with God and to assert that he was divine.

The Greek word for Lord – will you kindly put up with it if I seem to show off a bit? – is *kurios* and this originally meant someone who occupied a position of authority, and was used for an 'owner' or a 'governor' or the 'head of a family'. Later it came to be a title of polite or even deferential address, corresponding to our 'sir'. Most important for my point here, it also came to be the word used in the Greek translation of the Old Testament (the Septuagint, as it is called) for the Hebrew 'Yahweh' or 'Jehovah', meaning God. As a result *kurios* became for Jews the Greek equivalent of God. To apply this title to Jesus was to convey the clear implication that he was divine.

It was a most extraordinary step for any Jew to take to impute divinity to any human being. To appreciate just how extraordinary, we have to bear in mind again that the Jews were strict monotheists and had been for centuries, passionately resentful of any suggestion that there might be any other God than their Jehovah. And yet here were Jews become Christians who were convinced that their Jesus was divine. What a daring assertion they were making. How startlingly unorthodox to be attributing to a man born of woman a position alongside the God of their fathers. I ask you, can you think of anything other than his known Resurrection from the dead that could have impelled them to take such a step? I can not.

It might be argued that the words and works of Jesus prior to Easter implied his deity; and that this sufficiently explains the later ascription of that status by his followers. But it is only too obvious that, prior to Easter, the disciples were distressingly slow to understand Jesus and his teaching in this field. They had come at length, it is true, to a rather halting acknowledgment of his Messiahship but not by any means of his divinity.

This required a further and revolutionary step of faith, as orthodox Jewish thought did not generally regard the Messiah as one who was divine. The long-awaited Messiah was to be a man specially chosen and specially endowed as the agent of God – but a man.

It may be that some, more discerning than the rest, had come to detect in Jesus implications of divinity; but, if so, even they would have been brought up short in their thinking along these lines by the disaster of the cross. For what makes the subsequent hailing of Jesus as divine most surprising is the fact that his life had come to such a close. No thought of his being divine could have survived in the mind of any of his followers after that. Believing him to be Messiah, they would consider it unthinkable that God should even allow him to die. For Jesus to die, therefore, was a serious enough blow to their ideas concerning Jesus and Messiahship. For him to die by crucifixion, according to the scriptures the most abhorrent of all deaths, would make it doubly certain to them that any notions of his Messiahship, never mind his deity, had been sadly mistaken. If Jesus had really been the Son of God as they had begun falteringly to believe, God undoubtedly would have rescued him from death and vindicated him before all eyes.

What, then, are we to make of the fact that they ascribed deity to a man who had been crucified to death? Can the explanation be anything other than that God had vindicated Jesus after all, vindicated him in his own way by raising him from the dead? The whole Book of Acts makes it plain that to the first Christians the cross on which Jesus died was an object of shame and horror which only the Resurrection had transformed. They worship Jesus not because of that cross but in spite of it. It was only the interpretation of the cross in the light of the Resurrection which led to that changed attitude to it which is to be seen, for example, if you care to refer to them, in the letter to the Philippians and in the Gospel according to St John, where the crucifixion itself is seen as a demonstration of the glory of God. Such a change could not have come about except through an unshakable certainty of the truth of the Resurrection.

It is worth remembering this, too: remarkable though it was, it was not simply a matter of those who had followed Jesus before his crucifixion somehow coming to hail him as Lord after it. The history is even more remarkable yet. The Christians took their astonishing doctrine of the deity of one who had been executed as a criminal and managed to prevail on large numbers of their countrymen to accept it.

To every convert Jesus became Lord. 'Jesus is Lord' was in fact the earliest creed of the church and in all likelihood was part of the confession of faith that new members made at their baptism. What a mighty revolution it involved for these converted Jews to think and speak of Jesus in such a manner. The suggestion, even while he lived, that Jesus was divine would have been more than sufficient to fill them with the utmost repugnance. The making of such a suggestion after he had been crucified must have filled them with a horror so great that most of them would be very reluctant to listen any further to anything the Christians might have to say. It is, therefore, a matter of arresting significance that so many who did somehow condescend to listen were, in spite of their angry prejudice, convinced and converted. They, too, must have been made very sure that Jesus was risen.

Dear Minister

I have to admit that you have been marshalling a lot of valid evidence and presenting a good case. I am considering your arguments carefully and rereading your letters. Have you made all the evidential points you want to make or is there anything else you think I ought to take into account?

Dear John

Here is another point I would like you to consider but I want to say first of all that so far as being evidence for the Resurrection is concerned, I would not attempt to put it into the same category as the other factors I have asked you to consider. Up till now the evidence does not, in my submission, admit of any other reasonable and satisfactory explanation save that Jesus really did rise from the dead. What I am going to put before you now, however, is more of the nature of back-up or confirmatory evidence in my opinion. I recognize that it could conceivably be explained apart from the Resurrection; but at the same time it may be of considerable value, especially for the Christian who will be able to find in it further corroboration of his belief in the Resurrection.

What I have in mind is the testimony offered by the pre-Resurrection Jesus. It is worth remembering – and, despite what I have just been

saying, this applies to sceptics and enquirers as well as to believers –
that it is the Resurrection of *Jesus* we are concerned with. The belief
that I and so many others hold and which I have been endeavouring to
commend to you is not the resurrection of any ordinary man but the
resurrection of someone who was unique and very special in his
uniqueness.

The sceptic may object that it is preposterous that any man should
rise from the dead. In a way I fully agree. But the point is that it is the
Resurrection of Jesus that is postulated by Christian faith, not that of
any man. Resurrection is admittedly a strange phenomenon to intrude
upon human history but when the person of whom it is reported is
such a one as Jesus, it becomes a phenomenon much less surprising.
For him, on the contrary, it seems fitting and – in retrospect – even
inevitable.

That was how it seemed to the disciples once it had occurred and
they had become convinced of its truth. Peter, for instance, in preaching
the first Christian sermon ever recorded said of Jesus, 'God raised him
from death . . . because it was impossible that death should hold him
prisoner' (Acts, chapter 2, verse 24).

You might wish to point out that I have already insisted that the
Resurrection took the disciples by surprise. So I did and I stand by
that. But what I said a line or two back was that they appreciated its
appropriateness, even its inevitability, *once it had occurred.* Any
expectation of Jesus rising from the dead was foreign to their thoughts
before it happened but once it had taken place, the essential rightness
of the event became apparent to them. With hindsight it now seemed to
them impossible that there could have been any other ending to Jesus'
story.

At our distance and with the perspective available to us, we are able
to see even more clearly than they were that there never was a man like
this man and that his person and his Resurrection are very much in
accord with each other. His uniqueness is undeniable. He alone in all
history, for instance, has been totally free from sin. Not that 'sinless'

is an adequate adjective with which to describe his life; for sinlessness is a somewhat negative term whereas the life of Jesus was not only empty of wrongdoing but also full of goodness. His teaching, too, was unique. 'Nobody has ever talked like this man' was the report brought back by the spies sent out by the chief priests and Pharisees (John chapter 7, verse 46), and their verdict has been confirmed by every generation that has known the gospel records. His deeds also indicated his uniqueness. Many and wonderful were his works of healing, sometimes of body, sometimes of mind, sometimes of spirit, sometimes all three together.

The very person of Jesus seems to me to present a challenge to recognize his Resurrection as something that was inevitable. If such as he had remained captive to death, would that not have been a denial that there was any moral basis to the universe? It seems to me, John, that it would certainly have made nonsense of the belief that God has any real part in the world.

If the Resurrection claim had been made of any other person known to history that would have been one thing. The fact that the claim was made of this unique person who was Jesus of Nazareth is another thing altogether.

While I am at it, John, I may as well mention something else which similarly may not be a piece of evidence likely to cut much ice with anyone sceptically disposed but is one that confirms and strengthens the belief of many who already believe – another feature that might well be written off as purely subjective by the doubter but which the believer feels sure is much more than that. I refer to the sense of the presence of the risen Jesus.

From the earliest Christian times men and women who have committed themselves in faith and in service to Jesus in the belief that he was risen from the dead, have felt conscious of the presence of Jesus with them in their journey though life. This has been much more than a consciousness of being inspired by the memory of a dead friend, or of being stimulated by his example as one might be stimulated by the example of a dead hero. It has been the conviction that they had entered into an intimate relationship with one who was really alive and personally active in time and space. Accompanying this conviction and apparently testifying to its validity there has often been an inrush of new moral power to their lives.

I have already discussed with you the tremendous change in outlook and in spirit that took place in the disciples over Easter weekend because of their conviction that Jesus was risen from the dead. The disciples, however, were altered not only emotionally but morally as well. From that time on they began to display qualities of a kind and to a degree that no one knowing them would have thought possible. It is no exaggeration to say that ordinary men became supermen. How is this to be explained, I ask you? It seems obvious that it was not just the consequence of a gritting of the teeth and a girding of the loins. They were clearly living lives that were beyond the reach of their unaided capacity. They were like men possessed.

I believe the truth is that they *were* 'possessed' – possessed by the living Christ. At the very least the change in their lives tallied with their belief that they were living in even closer fellowship with him than before his crucifixion.

The same phenomenon was much in evidence throughout the early church. Whenever people came to have faith in the Risen Jesus, their lives began to show unmistakable signs of a new element having been added to their moral strength. Could this have come from any other source than the Risen Christ with whom they believed they were living in constant fellowship?

Nor has this phenomenon of Christian experience been merely temporary. Ever since, in every age, there have been thousands of men and women who have been conscious that the Risen Jesus was with them and whose lives have borne witness to the energizing influence of fellowship with him.

In our own day, too, there are lives that speak of new moral strength through the Risen Lord. Probably there were never more such witnesses than now. All over the world in greater numbers and in more places than ever before, there are men and women sure that the Risen Jesus is with them constantly, and able and willing to testify that since they committed themselves to the Christian faith a new moral factor entered their lives and changed them, often radically, for the better.

From the outset, then, Christians have felt aware of Jesus' presence, invisible but real; and many thousands of Christian lives have seemed to suggest strongly the possession of such moral energy and power as to demand explanation in something beyond themselves. Admittedly, as I inferred when I introduced the subject, it may well be objected, 'This "awareness" of the presence of Jesus could be no more than a subjective feeling brought about by their belief in his Resurrection' – and no one could disprove that contention. The objector might say again, 'All these instances of moral transformation you speak of might well be explained as the psychological consequence of the conviction that Jesus is alive and that his spirit is active' and again I must admit that the contention can not be disproved.

I freely admit, and was at pains to make the admission when I began this letter, that what I have been putting forward for consideration here is evidence different in kind from things like the birth and survival of the Christian church, the empty tomb and so on. The testimony of Christian experience and that of the person of Jesus do not have the same objectivity as items of evidence. Neither testimony may, however, be summarily dismissed on that account. They could, perhaps, be more readily disregarded if they stood alone. But they stand alongside a mass of more objective evidence which, I have been pleading, points unmistakably to the fact of the Resurrection.

And so, while what I have been saying in this letter may not constitute primary testimony and is likely to make little impression on the out-and-out sceptic, the Christian is entitled to find in it confirmation of his Resurrection belief.

Dear Minister

I confess that I have actually been considerably impressed by the evidence you have mustered in support of the truth of the Resurrection and also by the arguments you have adduced. Nevertheless, I still can't help feeling that there must be a more acceptable explanation of the facts than a Resurrection from the dead, even when Jesus of Nazareth is the person supposed to have been raised. Anything other than that, my mind protests; it is just too extraordinary to accept.

Dear John

I would counter the closing sentence of your last letter by saying that in my opinion it is even more extraordinary not to accept the Resurrection as true in view of the evidence for it.

In our correspondence I have been attempting to demonstrate how factor piling upon factor makes that truth sure. As I see it, it is impossible to explain in any really feasible way apart from its truth the Resurrection belief on which the Christian church was founded.

The real onus of making good their case in regard to the historicity or otherwise of Jesus' Resurrection rests surely not with those who believe it but with those who deny it. Those who believe it, after all, are accepting what the written records affirm and what the Christian church has always maintained. It is the unbeliever who is out of step and at variance with things as they are. If he is to justify his rejection of the Resurrection belief, it is up to him, is it not, to put forward a satisfactory alternative explanation as to how that belief arose and how it managed to survive and even to spread. The belief is there. That is a fact plain for all to see; and its existence, an existence which dates back to the beginning of the church, is a presumption in favour of its truth. That presumption must be counted sufficient to carry the day unless a convincing 'natural' explanation is forthcoming.

I have been trying to demonstrate in my letters to you, John, that there is no convincing alternative explanation. This leaves us with the inevitable conclusion that the Resurrection must be true.

It may bring the point home with fuller force if you adopt the position that Jesus did not rise from the dead and, having assumed that standpoint, proceed to try to fashion an explanation for the various factors relevant to the case – the origin of the belief, the transformation of the disciples, the writing of the Gospels, the empty tomb, the appearances of the Risen Jesus, the existence of the Christian church, and so on. It is my opinion that this will prove an impossible task. That being so, the implications are clear. It is the simplest of propositions that if an alleged fact is not false it must be true.

I am not unmindful of the fact that there have been many attempts to find 'other' explanations – and you have been having a go at this exercise yourself – but it seems to me that none of the alternatives offered comes anywhere near being convincing. It is, incidentally, quite interesting to observe how efficient a job these alternative theories often making of slitting one another's throats.

I would not claim that in the course of this correspondence between us I have put forward all the arguments and all the evidence that could be put forward in support of the Resurrection. I hope, though, that I have at least let you see that there is a strong case for accepting the Resurrection as a true fact of history. So often – very sadly, to my way of thinking – people imagine that to believe in the Resurrection necessitates a suspension of all one's critical faculties and a desperate ignoring of reality. I am reminded of the schoolboy who was asked to define 'faith' and gave this as his answer: 'Faith is believing in what you know is not true'.

A considerable number have that kind of view of the Christian faith and of the Resurrection in particular. I hope I may have said enough to let you see that it is not at all like that. Whether or not you choose to align yourself with the Easter belief, it can not reasonably be disputed that it has a lot going for it. Many people have been greatly surprised to discover this.

Frank Morrison is a well-known example. A journalist who reckoned that the Resurrection story was a lot of rubbish and ought to be exposed as such, he decided to write a book to do just that. In order to execute his task properly he felt that he must research his subject very thoroughly, and did so. Once his careful and extensive research was finished, he wrote his book all right, but it was not the book he had intended or expected to write, debunking the Resurrection. Instead it was a book advocating the truth of the Resurrection story because his study of the subject had convinced him that it must be true. His book, entitled *Who Moved the Stone?*, became a religious bestseller.

Admittedly the Resurrection can not be proved in the way that some things can be proved. It is not open, for instance, to the sort of proof that a laboratory experiment may be able to provide. But it has a great many factors in its favour; and it is well worth asking ourselves how many facts of history acknowledged as absolutely certain could be capable of absolute proof. For the Resurrection there is such a convergence of historical probabilities as to place its historicity beyond all reasonable doubt and this is the best that can be done for most matters of accepted historical truth.

It was my personal realization, after much study and not a little mental agonizing, of the strength of the evidence for the Resurrection – as constituted by this accumulation of probabilities – that constrained me to believe it true and so to become a Christian.

Dear Minister

I note your statement that the evidence for the Resurrection constrained you to believe it true 'and so to become a Christian'. Do I take from that that becoming a Christian is to be equated with believing in the Resurrection? Could I, then, not be a Christian unless I believed that Jesus had been raised from the dead?

Dear John

I am so glad that you raised the point you did in your last letter. It gives me the opportunity to attempt to clear up what I am afraid I left unclear when I said what I did linking my acceptance of the Resurrection belief with my acceptance of Jesus as my Saviour and Lord.

There are two things I must now try to explain.

The first is that belief in the Resurrection of Jesus does not of itself make anyone a Christian. Not all who believe that Jesus was raised from the dead are necessarily committed to Jesus and his way. The Devil, for example, knows jolly well that Jesus is risen but that does not make him a Christian. In my own case, because of my previous doubts about it, belief in the Resurrection was the necessary preliminary to my decision to let Jesus be my Lord and Master. It was, however, no more than a preliminary. I had to take a further step of trust and commitment.

Let me tell you a story I used to tell my intending new communicants during the weeks I tried to prepare them for full church membership. It is related of Blondin the famous stuntman of a past generation that on a certain occasion he wheeled a man in a barrow across a wire stretched perilously over Niagara Falls with a large spellbound crowd looking on. In the forefront of the crowd was a boy gazing in open-mouthed wonder at this astonishing feat. Noticing him, Blondin said,

'Did you enjoy the performance?' 'Oh yes,' was the answer. Blondin went on, 'Do you believe that I could wheel you across?' 'Oh, yes,' said the lad without hesitation. Having heard much of Blondin's prowess beforehand and having now seen it demonstrated before his own eyes, he had not the slightest doubt that Blondin could indeed do just that. 'Well, then,' continued Blondin, 'step into the barrow and I'll take you across in it.' But this was a vastly different kettle of fish and the boy declined.

He believed all right that Blondin could do it but he was not prepared to entrust his life to him nevertheless.

That story roughly illustrates the difference there is between having a conviction that Jesus was raised from the dead and having faith in the risen Christ. To be a Christian is not only to believe that Jesus is risen from the dead and alive today. Christian faith requires the taking of a further step, one that depends on that belief but that takes us far beyond it and involves the committing of ourselves in total surrender to the living Christ.

The second thing is this. Personally, I firmly believe that Jesus was raised from the dead in such a fashion that his human body was involved and his grave was left empty. As I see it, the facts do not reasonably admit of any other understanding. I am, however, well aware that there are some who are genuinely committed to Jesus Christ and his way who regard his Resurrection as purely a survival of his spirit. Whether or not the body of Jesus was involved in that survival is a matter of indifference to them; they consider it enough to believe that his spirit continues active in the world.

I find it difficult to understand how they can equate this position with a number of the factors I have been discussing with you and in my opinion that position is untenable from any standpoint that takes serious account of these factors. At the same time I would not dispute the sincerity of their allegiance to Jesus, to the Risen Jesus indeed and to their full entitlement to the name Christian. I might, and I do, regret that they do not quite see things my way and am saddened that they do not but I am sure that Jesus does not turn his back on them because of that.

Dear Minister

As I have already admitted, you make out a very good case for the truth of the Resurrection; but when all is said and done, does it really matter very much whether or not Jesus rose from the dead? After all, is the main thing not that the teaching of Jesus should be known and followed? Surely we do not need to believe in his Resurrection for that?

Dear John

Yet again I am grateful to you for bringing up important points and giving me the opportunity to say something about them. Again I think there are two lines I would like to follow in an attempt to answer your last question.

First, as a matter of history, had it not been for the Resurrection, there is no way the world would ever have got to know the teaching of Jesus. If the crucifixion had been the end of him, Jesus himself would speedily have been forgotten and his influence on others completely dissipated. Without his Resurrection his teaching would not have been perpetuated in any degree.

At the time, on that day we now call Good Friday, Jesus' crucifixion was total and seemingly irretrievable disaster. That was how it appeared to the disciples anyway. The whole enterprise was at an end. Jesus was dead and that was that.

Had that really been the end, nothing is more sure than that Jesus would never even have been heard of outside his own country, and very little even there outside of his own lifetime. It needed the Resurrection to give him and his teaching to the world.

There is a story I am fond of which I would like to share with you here. It may be quite apocryphal – I don't know – but it is a good story just the same. It tells that news of the Battle of Waterloo was brought by sailing ship to the south coast of England. By prearrangement a group of watchers was gathered on the shore waiting. In due course the ship came in sight and dropped anchor in full view of the watchers on the shore. Then the signaller began to spell out his message to them letter by letter – W.E.L.L.I.N.G.T.O.N. D.E.F.E.A.T.E.D. At that moment a blanket of fog descended suddenly upon the ship wrapping it away from the sight of those on the shore. But they thought the message was completed anyway and so the word was spread that the battle had been lost, creating gloom and despondency far and wide. After a time the sun broke through again and the fog was dispersed revealing the vessel once more to sight. Those few who had lingered on the shore, perhaps too brokenhearted to move, saw that the signaller was at work again; and this time he spelled out his complete message: W.E.L.L.I.N.G.T.O.N. D.E.F.E.A.T.E.D. T.H.E. E.N.E.M.Y. They could scarcely believe it for very joy; but it was true, and soon the whole country was resounding with the gladness of apparent defeat becoming actual victory.

It was in not dissimilar fashion that the news of Jesus' Resurrection broke upon the world. On Good Friday the stark outline of a cross upon a hill and the cold finality of a sealed grave proclaimed to all beholders a message that read JESUS DEFEATED. All weekend that was the message that hammered mercilessly and persistently upon the minds and spirits of Jesus' followers. Then came Easter morning when an empty tomb and a Risen Christ delivered the complete message: JESUS DEFEATED THE ENEMY; and gloom gave way to gladness.

It was not that the Resurrection was an overcoming of the cross. It was not a case of the crucifixion being a defeat which the Resurrection reversed. The crucifixion and the Resurrection were each part of the one story of victory; but it was the Resurrection that established the victory and proclaimed it. Without the Resurrection the story would have been one of defeat and failure. If Jesus had remained dead, his teaching would not have survived for any length of time.

The second thing to be said is that without the Resurrection and the consequent assistance made available to Jesus' followers through the power of His risen presence with them, no one could have lived out His teaching with any real measure of success even if it had been remembered. Most people, I imagine, would readily admit that the moral teaching of Jesus is the loftiest the world has ever known. But it is one thing to know the highest, it is usually quite another thing to achieve it. Christians believe they are assisted by the attendant spirit of the risen Jesus towards a closer approach to the ideals He set out than would be at all within their unaided grasp. In this regard, too, the Resurrection is of first importance.

I remember, in the long ago days of my youth, hearing a foreign missionary, home on furlough, tell a parable kind of story which greatly impressed me. A man walking through a jungle suddenly fell into a deep pit, set as a trap for unwary animals. Try as he might he was unable to climb out. The sides of the pit were too steep and too crumbly to afford him the hand- and footholds that he needed. After a while a moral philosopher chanced that way and when he observed the unfortunate traveller trapped in the pit, he stopped and pointed out where the poor man had strayed from the proper path and so caused his fall into the pit. But he was unable to help the prisoner escape. Shortly afterwards another philosopher came that way. He, too, stopped and commiserated with the wretched captive, still struggling desperately but in vain to make his way out of the pit. But he was able to offer no more help than to advise the prisoner on the route he should follow once he did manage his way to freedom. Later still, Jesus happened along, carrying his cross. Seeing the man in the pit, he lowered his cross down into the pit and when the trapped man took hold of the cross, Jesus was able to pull him to the surface. Having done that, he not only indicated the proper road to take but accompanied the man he had rescued as he went along that road.

I do not need to spell out what that story is meant to teach. I simply leave it with you to be chewed over.

Dear Minister

I am grateful to you for taking so much time and trouble with my doubts and reservations about the Resurrection. Your comments have helped me a lot towards an understanding of the Christian case and to a fuller understanding of why you and Christians in general are such firm believers in Jesus' rising from the dead. I no longer think of that belief, as I once did, as a lot of nonsense, either the figment of someone's overheated imagination or else the greatest hoax in history, but certainly something that was too absurd to be given serious consideration. I now realize there is a lot more to it than that.

I must also say, however, that I am still not convinced, not completely at any rate. I realize that there are a lot of strong arguments in favour of the truth of the Resurrection and I realize, too, that there are a number of things which are very, very difficult to explain if the Resurrection did not take place. On the other hand, I also find it very difficult still to believe that such an extraordinary event could ever have happened. I hope you are not too disappointed to hear this after all the trouble you have taken and which I do appreciate.

Dear John

I am disappointed, I must admit, that I have not (yet) succeeded in persuading you of the truth of the Resurrection but I am certainly not disappointed in you. On the contrary I am delighted that you have been so willing to give serious consideration to the various arguments I have been putting forward in answer to your questions.

It is so important in the approach to this question, as indeed in the approach to any question, to be as open-minded as possible and willing to consider all the relevant evidence fairly whether or not it is agreeable to one's predispositions and prejudices. Many, unfortunately, do not seem able to come to the question of the Resurrection with this kind of open-mindedness. They have such a deep-seated conviction that such an event is so unusual as to be absolutely impossible. Miracles, they are sure, do not happen, never did happen, can not happen. The Resurrection, therefore, the most miraculous of all miracles, can not possibly be countenanced; and so the evidence is never given a proper hearing. It is simply set aside as having no possible bearing on the conclusion to be reached.

It is, however, arbitrary and unjustifiable to conclude categorically that miracles can not happen and never did happen. It may sometimes be claimed that it is the modern world's scientific outlook that compels this conclusion. But it is, in fact, unscientific to make such a declaration. The most that science would be entitled to do, were it so minded, would be to state that it had not encountered a proven case of miracle. Some are bound to say, nevertheless, 'Whatever might be the evidence for it, I will refuse to believe in the Resurrection because I know it to be an impossibility.'

I am reminded of a story which harks back to the old educational days (my days) of learning multiplication tables by rota. You may have heard of those far-distant times and habits. You started off with the 2-times table – 2 times 2 are 4, 2 times 3 are 6, up to 2 times 12 are 24 – and ascended gradually to the dizzy heights of the 12-times table, culminating in the pinnacle of achievement which was to recite triumphantly 12 times 12 are 144. This was as far as the printed tables in our books went and as far, therefore, as this particular exercise proceeded. One little girl was one day being taken through her tables by her grandfather, and doing rather well. '6 times 6' she was asked and came back triumphantly with '36.'

'9 times 9?' was the next question and '81' came back at once; '12 times 12?' was just as swiftly answered with '144'. Then mischievously, grandfather said, '13 times 13?' She turned on him scornfully and said, obviously pitying his ignorance, 'Grandfather, there is no such thing'.

But, of course, there was such a thing, as you and I well know, but it lay outside that little girl's experience and she concluded, therefore, that it did not exist. That story may illustrate my point that the mere fact of something never having entered our experience is not sufficient ground for assuming that it can not exist. If a supposed 'scientific' outlook hinders anyone from accepting the Resurrection belief, he is as well to know that most scientists today would readily concede that miracle is not a scientific impossibility and that every alleged instance of it should be judged solely on the evidence.

Miracles (and the Resurrection in particular) could properly be written off as impossible only if it could be proved that there is no God. If a man believes in God's existence, there is for him no reasonable obstacle to his believing that miracles are possible and so, of course, the Resurrection. Even where a man does not believe in God's existence, so long as he has to admit the possibility of that existence – so long, in other words, as he is unable to prove that God does not exist – so long must he admit the possibility of miracle. Since, therefore, it is impossible to disprove the existence of God (no matter how much it may be doubted or disbelieved), the possibility of miracle – and particularly, for our purposes, of the Resurrection – can never be entirely ruled out.

Which brings us back to my earlier contention that the only legitimate question concerning the historical truth of the Resurrection is whether or not the evidence is strong enough to justify belief in it.

It brings us back, too, to the pleasure I expressed at the attitude you have been showing to this discussion we have been conducting by letter. Whether or not you ever come to feel that the evidence for the Resurrection is sufficiently compelling for you, you have all along been prepared to consider it as fairly and as honestly as you are able. I say 'as your are able' for none of us can ever shake free entirely from prejudice and bias. This makes your open-mindedness all the more creditable.

Dear Minister

Thank you for your kind words. I am not quite there so far as accepting the Resurrection belief is concerned but I am certainly a lot nearer to it than I was when this series of letters began. I am still turning over in my mind many of the things you have said and still seeking, I must confess, some satisfactory explanation other than the one you advocate. Meantime, I would be interested to have you tell me, if you will, something of the difference it makes to the Christian to believe that Jesus was raised from the dead.

Dear John

I am only too pleased to respond to your invitation to tell you something of what the Resurrection of Jesus means to the Christian believer.

I should probably reiterate first of all that to the Christian the Resurrection is the most important event in all human history; for the very simple reason that the whole structure of the Gospel depends upon it. If the Resurrection is true, the Gospel is real; if the Resurrection is false, the Gospel collapses. Writing in the early days of the church, the Apostle Paul said this very thing in these words; 'If Christ has not been raised from death, then we have nothing to preach and you have nothing to believe' (1 Cor. 15.14) The Resurrection is the keystone of the Christian faith, and was at one and the same time the cause and the motive and central affirmation of the preaching of the apostles.

That is why it would be out of the question for me, as you once advised me to do, to abandon preaching the Resurrection since so many find it a stumbling-block. As you did, many people ask, 'Why not just preach the simple Gospel and leave out the supernatural bits? These are what so many can not stomach.' The answer is that, if the Resurrection is taken away, no Gospel remains. The Gospel, which means literally 'the Good News', was, in the beginning and still is, that Jesus who was crucified is risen from the dead. There never was a Gospel independent of the Resurrection; the Christian faith and its proclamation are essentially linked to Jesus' Resurrection. A M Ramsey, a former Archbishop of Canterbury, says in his book, *The Resurrection of Christ*, (p 7), 'For them (the New Testament Christians) the Gospel without the Resurrection was not merely a Gospel without its final chapter; it was not a Gospel at all.'

What you are asking about, however, is the significance of the Resurrection for the Christian. If I were to put that significance into one word, the word I would have to choose would be 'Victory'. What happened at the first Easter was that Jesus was raised victorious from the grave, establishing victory not only over death itself but, as the Bible expresses it, also over 'all the powers of darkness'; and the victory is one that Jesus is able and eager to share with anyone and everyone who is willing to accept a share in it.

Let me try to spell out the significance of the Resurrection in a little more detail. If in so doing I sound as if I have ascended the pulpit, please try to forgive me.

The Resurrection means, for one thing, that Jesus' cause is one that can never finally be defeated. Whatever the picture may be at any given time, ultimate victory is assured for Jesus and his way. However it may seem in our own day or in any other day, the Resurrection proclaims emphatically and irrefutably that good is stronger than evil and love stronger than hate; and that in the end these must prevail. To put it otherwise, those who align themselves on the side of Christ have taken their stand on the winning side, for the Resurrection has made it certain that somehow, sometime, God will consummate his kingdom.

This assurance can be a source of great encouragement and consolation when the world and society are passing through dark and troubled times and when evil seems to be in the ascendancy all along the line. The words of AH Clough's poem, which was once in our Church of Scotland hymnbook, may be used to express something of the confidence felt in this regard by one who believes in the Resurrection.

> 'Say not – the struggle nought availeth,
> The labour and the wounds are vain,
> The enemy faints not, nor faileth –
> And as things have been, they remain!
>
> For while the tired waves, vainly breaking,
> Seem here no painful inch to gain,
> Far back, through creeks and inlets making,
> Comes silent – flooding in – the main.
>
> And not by eastern windows only,
> When daylight comes, comes in the light;
> In front the sun climbs slow – how slowly!
> But westward – look! the land is bright.'

The Resurrection has significance for the Christian not only in this broader sense but also in relation to his own personal life. For it gives the promise of victory there, too, victory over all the dark and hurtful things that may, and often do, enter into human experience, victory over everything that tends to spoil life at its best.

It means, for one thing, victory over loneliness. After his Resurrection, Jesus said to his disciples, 'Be assured. I am with you always,' and, like all his promises, this is one he keeps. The Christian, therefore, need never feel lonely because he is never alone. His risen Lord is always close beside him. In my first charge in Newmilns, Ayrshire, I used to visit regularly an old widowed lady who had lived all by herself for the past thirty years in an attic at the top of a flight of rather steep stairs which for years past she had been unable to negotiate without help. She was, consequently, hardly ever out of her house but her spirit remained indomitably bright. On one of my visits she said to me, 'You know, Mr Martin, people think I must be terribly lonely living up here all by myself. But I never feel lonely because, you see, I'm never alone. The Master is always beside me.'

For the Christian the Resurrection of Jesus also spells victory over sin. Sin is one of the chief enemies of life at its best and the risen Jesus offers two-fold triumph over sin. He offers both the opportunity to have our sins forgiven through faith in him and also the opportunity to be given strength to overcome them. Given the chance, the risen Jesus can make new men and new women of us, even of the most unlikely of us, just as he did with his disciples in the immediately post-Easter days and as he has done with so many people since.

Sin is not much spoken of nowadays, not by that name at any rate. Sin is not a popular term at the present time but there is still a lot of it around. We may use other terms like maladjustment and going off the rails and we may speak of environmental and hereditary tendencies and the like but the hurt and sorrow human wickedness causes are none the less for that. The world at large today, our immediate society and our individual lives tell harrowing tales of the damage sin can cause. One aspect of the message of Jesus' Resurrection is that he has defeated sin and he invites us to avail ourselves through faith in him of the resources to defeat it also. Through taking up that invitation individual lives can be improved, society can be cleansed of much that disfigures it and even the world can be made into a better place.

The Resurrection means also that through faith in the risen Jesus, victory is available over trouble and disaster. An awareness of the companionship of their living Lord is able to keep Christians from being defeated by the disappointments and difficulties and frustrations of ordinary days and able even to raise them triumphant over the major disasters of tragedy and heartbreak that may come their way.

Another aspect of the victory gained for mankind by the Resurrection of Jesus is victory over fear. Fear is perhaps one of the most crippling things to enter into human experience. No one who is in the grip of fear can possibly be enjoying life in anything like full measure. To be afraid is to have the bloom stripped from our lives and there are many things calculated to strike fear into human hearts – things like illness and pain, unemployment and poverty, loneliness and bereavement, death and dying, and the threat of them and of many another. Christian faith does not remove the fearsome things of life from our path. Jesus never promised that it would. On the contrary he was at pains to give warning that following him would not make life easier. Believing in the Resurrection and in the risen Christ does not enable us to bypass the things that make men and women afraid but it will provide the courage and the strength to face up to them without fear because they are assured that there is nothing in all the world that has the power to defeat them now that they are invested with the power of the Risen Christ. The knowledge of his presence with them can produce a serenity of mind and spirit which is stronger than fear. Jesus said once to his followers: 'In the world you will have trouble. But courage. The victory is mine; I have conquered the world' (John chapter 16, verse 33). With this promise in mind, no Christian of any age need be afraid of anything.

Leslie Weatherhead tells in one of his books of visiting a friend of his in hospital who was terminally ill with cancer. He knew and she knew that she was soon to die and he found it difficult to say what was in his heart to say. But suddenly she, who had always been quiet and reticent about her faith, surprised him. 'Don't be troubled about me,' she said, 'I know that what you preach is true and I am not afraid.' Weatherhead said in reply, 'My dear, perhaps you are not going to get better of your cancer, but you have certainly conquered it.'

Men and women of Christian faith will be buffeted by life's storms just as severely, sometimes more so, as the unbeliever. But because of their relationship with the Risen Christ, they know that there is nothing that can finally defeat them – either of life or of death. For, of course, the Resurrection victory offered the Christian to share in is victory over death, too. As the Saviour conquered death, so will his followers. That is part of our Christian faith and part of the significance of what took place at the first Easter. DL Moody, the famous American evangelist, once remarked to a group of friends, 'Some morning you may read in the newspapers that DL Moody is dead. When you do, don't believe it. At that moment I will be more alive than I am now.' This part of Christian faith is exultantly expressed in that hymn which is a favourite of mine:

'Thine be the glory – risen, conquering Son,
Endless is the victory thou o'er death hast won'

and especially, in the present context, the last verse:

'No more we doubt thee, glorious Prince of Life;
Life is naught without thee; aid us in our strife;
Make us more than conquerors, through thy deathless love:
Bring us safe through Jordan to thy home above.'

Dear Minister

You speak so confidently about the victory Christians share in with the risen Jesus. I respect your sincerity but I am bound to say that I don't observe so much of this triumphant gladness in many of the Christians I know. Why should that be, I wonder. How would you go about explaining that?

Dear John

Point taken.

I, too, observe in some Christians much less than there should be of the triumphant gladness of which I was speaking and which, I believe, ought to characterize every true follower of Jesus Christ. The reason for the difference between the possible and the actual is that Christians do not always take up in full measure the victory Jesus offers to them.

I have a fairly old book on my shelves, written by a man called Fullerton, in which he tells of visiting the village of Domodossala in the Italian Alps. On the hill behind the village a series of little chapels had been built, climbing up the hillside in ascending order. They depicted with life-size terracotta figures various scenes from the Passion of Jesus, one, for instance, representing Jesus before Pilate, another showing him shouldering his cross, and so on. Fullerton made pilgrimage through these Passion tableaux, visiting each shrine in turn and climbing higher and higher up the hillside as he did so. Eventually he came to the Chapel of Calvary and found himself looking upon the figure of Jesus hanging on the cross. Up to this point the pathway between the shrines was well-worn by the feet of the countless pilgrims who had come, like Fullerton, to look upon these representations of Jesus' sufferings and death.

But Fullerton noticed that, though the path continued upwards beyond the Chapel of Calvary, it was from here on grass-grown and obviously little used. He, however, followed it on. It took him right to the summit of the hill and there he came to the climax of it all, the Chapel of the Resurrection, representing the empty tomb and the risen Christ. Comparatively few pilgrims, it was clear, took the trouble to visit it. The builders of those shrines had not forgotten that the crucified Jesus had been raised from the dead but most of the visitors, it would appear, came to pay homage to a Jesus who, for all practical purposes, was dead.

A number of Christians seem, regrettably, to stop short in similar fashion at Calvary. For them Easter is not the day it should be in the calendar of their faith. They know that Jesus is risen and alive. They do not doubt or disbelieve it. But the belief somehow has not become fully part of them and they seem not to appreciate properly that it means that Jesus is really alive and their constant, though invisible, companion.

There is an old story but a true one which may be worth repeating to you. A famous Congregationalist minister of a past generation, R W Dale, has recounted how he was working one day on his sermon for Easter when suddenly the significance of his chosen theme caught hold of his mind in a fashion that it had never done before. He leaped to his feet in excitement and began pacing up and down his study floor, halting every now and then to embrace afresh the new insight that had come to him. Let me quote you his own words: '"Christ is alive," I said to myself, "Alive!" and then I paused – "Alive! Can that really be true? Living as really as I myself am?" At first it seemed strange and hardly true, but at last it came upon me as a burst of sudden glory; yes, Christ is living. It was to me a new discovery. I thought all along I had believed it; but not until that moment did I feel sure about it.'

His book goes on to testify that from that moment on his life possessed a new quality and a new joy. Many Christians, perhaps, who are totally convinced that the Resurrection is true, nevertheless need to make the same kind of discovery that its truth is very relevant to their daily lives. Too often it may appear to many Christians as just another doctrine which, although absolutely true, does not have much significance for the actual business of modern-day living. It is not doubted but neither is it doubted that Elizabeth was Queen of England at the time of the Spanish Armada and the one belief affects the manner in which they put through their daily lives little more than the other.

Some Christians appear to lack a real awareness that the Jesus in whose Resurrection they firmly believe is actually alive and active, though unseen. No more astonishing message was ever announced to the world than that the crucified felon, Jesus of Nazareth, had been raised from the dead and was alive again – too astonishing for some to believe despite the evidence supporting it. It is no less astonishing today but I assure you once more, John, that it is really true; and I assure you also that it makes all the difference in the world to live one's life in the awareness that it is true.